JUST
WATCH ME

JUST WATCH ME

REMEMBERING PIERRE TRUDEAU

LARRY ZOLF

James Lorimer & Company, Publishers
Toronto 1984

ISBN 0-88862-735-1 cloth
      0-88862-734-3 paper

Cover and text design: Don Fernley.
Photo sections design: N. R. Jackson.
All photos reproduced courtesy of Canapress Photo Service except final photo in Chapter 5 (Howard Kay) and back cover (Gail Harvey).

Canadian Cataloguing in Publication Data

Zolf, Larry.
      Just watch me: remembering Pierre Trudeau

1. Trudeau, Pierre Elliott, 1919- 2. Canada -
Politics and government - 1963- I. Title.

FC626.T78Z64 1984   971.064'4'0924   C84-098769-2
      F1034.3.T78Z64 1984

James Lorimer & Company, Publishers
Egerton Ryerson Memorial Building
35 Britain Street
Toronto, Ontario M5A 1R7

Printed and bound in Canada
6 5 4 3 2 1 84 85 86 87 88 89

Contents

Preface   VII

1 The Politics of My Way   1

2 The Sexual Combat of the Single Warrior   17

3 More Elliott than Trudeau?   29

4 The Movable Feast of Canadian Salon Socialism   40

5 Meltdown in the Melting Pot   61

6 Succession Duties   82

Preface

I must confess that I have more than a vested interest in Pierre Elliott Trudeau. For the past twenty-one years, since the first time I met Trudeau, he has been a bit of a cottage industry for me. First of all, we worked together as TV reporters and commentators; then when he was the prime minister, I was presented for inspection before he graciously agreed to be interviewed.

I was also probably the only mischief-maker Trudeau approved of or respected. On two occasions I wrote for him detailed, scabrous speeches to be delivered to the assembled drunks, dinosaurs and dunces of the Parliamentary Press Gallery. Though these feeble efforts of mine were invariably botched by the Prime Minister, they were the only times he made anyone laugh at these irreverent occasions.

Trudeau, of course, was best at wit, namely at put-down, insult, verbal vendettas and so on. Here, of course, Trudeau did not need my help. Most Canadians like neither wit nor humour; and in these essays I hope I have obliged them to the full. After all, the Trudeau phenomenon is a serious matter and must be approached with the utmost of gravity. This collection of essays will never be classified as "humorous" or indeed "informative." Too many critics will dismiss them as tendentious, as lacking footnotes, or the sponsorship of a serious economic or academic body.

To all this I plead guilty. Had my publisher, James Lorimer, not asked me to disgorge my treasure chest of Trudiana, I would

today have been busy working on *Trough Luck*, the life story of
James Coutts, or *The Whalen Wall*, the life story of Eugene "Hat
Trick" Whelan. Mr. Lorimer seemed to feel that my many years
as a journalist, in and out of Trudeau court, were sufficient guarantees of my coming up with something readable about Canada's
fifteenth prime minister.

Hopefully these essays fit into Mr. Lorimer's fitful mandate;
to write them I have relied on what I have learned from many
conversations over the years with P.E.T. himself and many of
his associates, not to mention most of the parliamentarians and
politicians that were heavily involved in the Trudeau years. I
have, of course, ploughed through voluminous amounts of speech
material, articles, memoirs and books about Trudeau and the
Trudeau years.

But while these essays reflect this material, I hope they are
not a mere condensation of it. They may, in many parts, be a
new way of looking at Trudeau. Some of them look at situations
and aspects of Trudeau sadly neglected or forgotten.

In no way is this book intended to be a definitive biography
of Pierre Trudeau. Nor does it cover all aspects of his career.
But it would be fair to say that P.E.T. would approve the format,
if not all of the content, of these essays. He should. The tone,
the temper and much of the structure reflects the influence on
me of the kind of essay writing that *Federalism and French
Canadians* has made famous. In an even more humble way, the
Trudeau essays, which readily tackled totems and taboos of their
time, encouraged me to believe that I could rightfully test some
of the favourite myths and nostrums that have attached themselves to P.E.T.

While these essays were not intended to be thigh-slappers and
most of the content is serious, I have taken careful steps to avoid
being deadly dull. I have chosen provocative areas and said
provocative things. Sometimes the taste of my tongue in my
cheek would last for hours. Feeble attempts at wit have occa-
sionally escaped by me and some humorous remarks do some-

times occur. For this I can only say that, for a Canadian, being funny is always having to say, I'm sorry. I'm sorry.

That my essays have some import, my favourite political guru, Christina McCall, has readily assured me after an early reading of my efforts. The Honourable Donald S. Macdonald was kind enough to read the manuscript, and made appropriate comments and corrections. Other prominent and well-meaning Canadians have read portions of my manuscript and pronounced those portions "serious." Public readings by me of this manuscript have quelled several disturbances in my neighbourhood and put even more apprehended insurrections to sleep. I sent it to then Prime Minister Trudeau, hoping this exercise in mutual vanity press would at last earn me my coveted senatorship.

I hasten to add that these essays reflect only my views — and certainly not Trudeau's, Christina McCall's or Donald Macdonald's. Well, perhaps not entirely my own views: in the pages to come, enterprising readers will find themselves face to face with a character glibly described as the Jaded Observer. Apart from having a splendid bulbous nose, a satanically stuffed belly, the eyesight of a Coke bottle bottom, the stick-to-itiveness of a Paul Hellyer, the overpreening ego of your average *Globe and Mail* reporter, the inferiority complex of a John Turner, and the sex life of a brontosaurus — the author and the Jaded Observer have absolutely nothing in common.

The Jaded Observer is simply the author's eyes and ears, and often his only friend; the Jaded Observer says things the more timorous author would not dare to. The author is aware the Jaded Observer is prettier and more popular than he is but shares to the fullest the J.O.'s conquests, verbal and otherwise. The author only calls on the Jaded Observer when it is that incredible hulk's inner views and inner eye that can best tell the story. The Jaded Observer is a bit of a braggart and a coward but he's always entertaining; sometimes he is even informative.

The author begs your indulgence for what the J.O. has to say; the J.O., of course, does not give a damn. This, to the author, seems perhaps an admirable partnership, one in which the author can double-deal and double his pleasures in telling the tale that is soon to unfold.

I would now like to thank P.E.T. for making all this possible. I can think of no other to thank, except perhaps Keith Davey for keeping Trudeau alive at the polls and Barbra Streisand, Liona Boyd, Margot Kidder and Sandra O'Neill, for keeping Trudeau alive period. I would also like to thank the banking community, the Liberal Party, the CBC, the Parliamentary Press Gallery, and the Toronto and Ottawa Press Clubs, for letting my shrivelled opus slip by them without comment.

I would also like to thank my editor, Ted Mumford (Mr. Patience himself), my publisher James Lorimer, my CBC colleague Colin McLeod and my Toronto Press Club business buddy, Fred Fraser, vice-president Canadian Aviation Electronics, for reading and commenting (always wisely) on everything I put before them; and my wife, Patricia, for being so cooperatively complacent about this whole affair.

Finally, this book is an unauthorized look at Pierre Trudeau — unauthorized by Trudeau and by anyone I know or work for. All complaints should, therefore, be sent to Larry Zolf, the Senate of Canada, Ottawa, Ontario, K1A 0A4.

If I am not there to answer these complaints, whose fault is that?

L.Z.
June 1984

1 The Politics of My Way

Unlike the United States, with its generalissimo politics — Washington, Jackson, Grant, Eisenhower — the martial arts have been conspicuously absent from Canadian politics. But there is one exception: in 1968 Pierre Elliott Trudeau became the first Canadian leader to bring the gunslinger-Lone Ranger ethos to Canadian politics.

Trudeau introduced to Canada the refined art of single combat; it was the politics of "Doing It My Way" — the politics of going my way or being left behind. Single-combat confrontation implied much more than the loner or renegade in power, and far far less than the shaman black tricks of Mackenzie King. Trudeau was always far more the solo Philosopher King engaged in intellectual trial by combat than the Magus Merlin conjuring up solutions by puffs of smoke, sleight of hand or divine intervention. Ouija-board politics was the occult domain of Mackenzie King, a man virtually devoid of policy, a political palm reader forever checking the whims and moods of his powerful baronial — Ralston, Howe, St. Laurent — and sometimes Byronian colleagues to see how best he could placate them, or calm them, or Heep his beatitudes upon them.

Trudeau, from day one, was always more samurai than shaman. Even in his pre-leadership days, Trudeau's love of trial by combat was predominant. Mackenzie King would have never touched the unholy trinity of divorce, abortion and homosexuality: each one of these issues is a sleeping dog best left to lie; each could

1

only infuriate conservative Canada from coast to coast. Since King dared not touch them seriatim he certainly would not have touched them together — in an omnibus bill.

This, Trudeau did joyously. The myth-makers have it that this was Trudeau's first deliberate joust, the kingship being the final prize. But Trudeau had no leadership aspirations at the time; all that he had, and still has, was the love of combat for the sake of combat and religious scruples be damned. Trudeau the Catholic zealot tackled divorce, abortion and homosexuality as moral and philosophical abstractions, piously playing the utopian Social Engineer blowing up the bridges and dams of social convention. It is ironic that Plaza Pierre, surely the most heterosexually active prime minister in this country's history, liberated the homosexual practitioners of black acts totally abhorrent to him; ironically, in the process, Trudeau gave irrational Canada a pretext for branding him a homosexual too.

P.E.T. has always hated the consensus building of a Mackenzie King; even the populist following of a Diefenbaker was an anathema to Trudeau. The single-combat warrior "doing it my way" is always alone; he leads the people but is not of them; like the prophet he wanders either in deserts or lush green pastures and often, like the prophet, he watches his people march into the Promised Land without him. For Trudeau, being alone is to be free; victory is a consequence of solitude; companionship an act of weakness, cronyism even worse.

It is again ironic that Trudeau, a devout Jansenist Roman Catholic, emotionally and philosophically opposed to both divorce and abortion, should grant Canadians greatly expanded divorce rights and their first right to a legal abortion.

Trudeau took on the unholy trinity then disturbing the bedrooms of the nation because all three were trial by combat, all three required one strong man to push them through. In this minefield Canada's political loner had walked alone and apparently loved it.

Canada's other solo flyer, John Diefenbaker, may or may not have been a renegade in power, but the input his politics received from Senate cronies and kitchen cabinets was enormous. The letters and advice that daily poured in to the Chief were a populist input that Diefenbaker slavishly adhered to. Trudeau was no Diefenbaker; he was neither a populist nor a renegade. Trudeau was simply a man who brilliantly massaged and manipulated others so that his single will appeared to be the will of many, so that his will be always done.

The theme of my-way politics sheds much light on the *vrai* Trudeau, the Trudeau that *is*, rather than the Trudeau people think there is. Trudeau has never been the privacy-demanding recluse, the reluctant leader that the herdsmen of Canadian journalism insist he is.

In secular life Trudeau is no trinitarian; he has chosen his oneness because, from his earliest politics, that oneness worked for him so spectacularly. Trudeau's personal handling of the conscription crisis was a "my way" all the way. Trudeau, the self-proclaimed socialist prophet of his people, waxed ever so eloquently against the sins of conscription, and yet Trudeau seemingly could not see in War Measures the potential greater evil of a Canadian fascism that surely meant permanent conscription and enslavement of all. Equally puzzling is the refusal of Trudeau's nationalist compatriots and colleagues in the years since to give him any credit for fighting in 1942 a good nationalist fight on behalf of the anti-conscription, quasi-separatist candidacy of Jean Drapeau; not so puzzling is the refusal of Anglo-Saxon patriots to give Trudeau any credit at all for joining a reserve regiment before the war. There was both a typical Trudeau "a plague on both your houses" in all this, and even more of the gunslinger spraying bullets on both sides of the saloon bar.

The style of the lone gunslinger was already apparent in Trudeau's early radical posture. *Cité libre* was a radical editorial collective run completely by Trudeau. Trudeau the then internationalist and socialist shared ideological bed and board with David Lewis, Frank Scott, Eugene Forsey and Thérèse Casgrain, but only Trudeau's CCF and NDP membership cards mysteriously do not exist today. Even that minor bit of collectivist discipline, the proud possession of a party card, was abhorrent to the free-wheeling independent Trudeau.

The ideologically committed gunslinger found little in the democratic process to nourish him. The social democrat Trudeau first entered the electoral lists only as a Liberal and only in the safest Liberal seat in the country. Trudeau knew that group dynamics, group participation, the democratic process where the many shape the few, is not as ideologically and politically effective as when the few shape the many.

This single-warrior syndrome explains many shifts and patterns in the Trudeau character. Diefenbaker revelled in the democratic panorama; Diefenbaker failed to keep urban Canada aboard his carousel and never really got French Canada to jump aboard in the first place, but the Chief's strengths and weaknesses flowed from the ordinary people who loved him and the sophisticates and big city people who hated him. P.E.T. never did deal in democratic norms; instead, the elitist Trudeau gave Quebec's elitists the first crack at the bilingual club and transformed the federal bureaucracy, at least on its highest levels, to a bilingual workplace in which the francophone would *de facto* be supreme.

In both of these basically undemocratic exercises, Trudeau was catering to Quebec's elites and Quebec's fellow single warriors. But the spectacle of naked, raw democracy in action, be it the staged Maple Leaf Gardens rallies where Trudeau flaunted his gunslinger stance, or the jam-packed crowds that watched him marshal the Calgary stampede, the elitist Trudeau also truly loved.

Despite the West's thorough rejection of Trudeau and all his works, Trudeau's love of the Wild Wild West was unequalled by any other prime minister. In still one more surprising contradiction Trudeau, who could see nothing but racism and yahooism in Western Canada, was still dazzled by the colourful costumes and traditions of the rugged individuals who live there.

One day a ferocious Trudeau stepped into the lobby of the House of Commons. There greeting him were the assembled paparazzi and pundits of Parliament Hill. Trudeau's fury cowed them into silence until the Jaded Observer, the cowardliest papar-

To make single-combat politics credible to the people, a newly elected Prime Minister Pierre E. Trudeau has to be gutsy.

In the face of bottle-hurling demonstrators at the 1968 St. Jean Baptiste Parade, Trudeau will not be moved. This magnificent exercise of physical courage makes Trudeau a national hero; English Canada forgives Trudeau's spotty war record and soon signs up for War Measures instead.

Sometimes the single-combat warrior is angry.

Or nutsy.

Sometimes the people are angry.

Or nutsy.

Sometimes the charismatic leader can't figure it all out, so he shrugs it off.

But in the end he always gets the people to pay attention...

. . . as he whistles while he works.

azzo of them all, cautiously enquired: "Excuse me, Prime Minister!" "What do you want?!!!" Trudeau shouted. "I just want to tell you how much I admire your cowboy suit," the Jaded Observer said.

Trudeau was fitted from top to bottom in Western gear. "Do you like it?" said the Prime Minister, ever eager for compliments of any kind on his Western demeanour; getting such a compliment from the Jaded Observer, Western Canada's most distinguished and best dressed paparazzo, was more than Trudeau could ever have counted on. "Did you get the stuff from Grand Saddlery on 8th Avenue in Calgary?" asked the Jaded Observer. By now Trudeau was doing his full roping, branding and bull steering repertoire in front of the Jaded Observer and the assembled paparazzi and punditi. Everyone had forgotten what to ask the Great Man; but from now on everyone could plainly see that in spirit at least Trudeau was as big a plainsman as Diefenbaker, who could no more rope, brand or bull steer than the Jaded Observer could stand tall in the saddle.

As fellow gunslingers, Westerners could relate to Trudeau, the single-combat warrior. Any man who single-handedly ropes a calf, busts a bronco and ties the horns of an angry bull, can understand Him who shoots the rapids alone and declares War Measures — alone. All gunfighters are selfish; the Western macho men could easily see their Eastern counterpart in Trudeau; and the Western single warrior, loving himself above all other men, could somehow understand Trudeau loving his Québécois above them. In 1968 a good slice of the Western macho pie went to P.E.T., the fastest gun in Quebec.

Trudeau in 1968 was unique not because he was Canada's first French Canadian philosopher king (which he was), but because Trudeau was the first French Canadian prime minister willing to confront and slug it out with his enemies (and sometimes his friends) in open battle. Few other Quebec politicians shared this Trudeau trait; my-way confrontational politics were not exactly a staple product of La Belle Province.

From the earliest beginnings of this country, the French experience had always been precarious; often it was marginal. Precarious, marginal experience breeds sharp, heightened responses; in some it causes a no-nonsense, *force majeure* posture which shuns compromise or consensus. The exposed position becomes the one true faith; better to go down in flames than to be smothered in feathers. The confrontationist-duellists of francophonia, Louis Riel, Louis Papineau, Henri Bourassa, the masters of ''let my people go,'' typify this aspect of the French Canadian character. The cautious magicians, the spinners of the abacus balls, the dealers in necessary-necessities, the pleaders of ''let my people stay'' — Laurier, King's French lieutenant Ernest Lapointe, St. Laurent — were a French Canadian leadership virtually invisible, and secondary in nature to the more elemental forces in French Canadian society, a francophone leadership that, before Trudeau, had kept Canada united for almost a century.

In this potent mix of race, creed and compromise Pierre Elliott Trudeau was the Fourth Horseman of the French Canadian apocalypse. The hobbyhorses Trudeau rode, linguistically and culturally, were new and vigorous. French rights outside Quebec as perceived by Laurier, Lapointe and St. Laurent were perhaps innate (although all three eschewed the espousal of the compact theory of Confederation in which Quebec supposedly entered as an equal partner). These rights had to be accepted widely before they could be effective. To these French Canadian gentlemen the winning over of English hearts to French rights was as important as, if not more important than, winning over the hearts and minds of the Quebec clergy and bourgeoisie. To the Four Horsemen, French rights were, like all Catholic insights, self-evident, natural rights, permanent and immanent, rights to be automatically deduced, rather than slowly induced.

Sometimes these forums of francophone leadership overlapped; sometimes they caused confusions and misreadings that bred bitter politics in their wake. Trudeau, for example, could only see Duplessis as the Black King, the crowned Uncle Tom of an enslaved people (Duplessis had supposedly done much to enslave). The next logical step for the Trudeau school of Quebec politics was to falsely conclude that Duplessis had no roots in Quebec, and that Trudeau and his socialist band were the particular wills that constituted the real general will of the Quebec people. The concept of One Canada flowed naturally from such a Trudeau appraisal. Duplessis, said the Trudeau forces, was corrupt, intolerant, reactionary, devoid of even a shred of modernism or progress in his makeup. Duplessis, of course, advocated an early version of Stanfield's ill-fated *Deux Nations*. In contrast Trudeau was modern, progressive, tolerant and, above all, free and rational; as such, Trudeau was for One Canada, a oneness reserved first for Trudeau's La Patrie, the province of Quebec, and then for the one world that global villageism was sure to bring.

Trudeau's contempt for the Liberalism of Laurier, Lapointe and St. Laurent was almost as marked as his contempt for Duplessis. Duplessis at least was vigorous, macho, certainly worthy of a duel for the hearts and minds of Quebec. Laurier et al were simply feather merchants, forever tickling noses and counting each sneeze as a triumph. Thus the One Canada policy of Trudeau emerged; the Laurier-Lapointe-St. Laurent policy respecting provincial jurisdiction in matters of language and culture was ceremoniously scrapped by Trudeau. The supporters of Trudeau, the relative Liberal arriviste, could in 1984 point a finger at life-long Liberals like Turner for espousing the provincial linguistic doctrines of Laurier and St. Laurent. The old traditionalist Liberals became the rock-the-boat-radicals in the confrontationist politics of Trudeau. The traditions and official concepts of Canadian Liberalism were now the exclusive preserve of Trudeau Liberals.

But the Trudeau victory was more apparent than real. The people of Manitoba in the language war of '84 were not alone; the people of Ontario, as in 1896, were not far behind them. Nor is the Trudeau reading of his own people holy writ throughout Quebec. The venal and corrupt Duplessis, the central voodoo symbolism in the Trudeau philosophy, is today the superstar of a Radio-Canada epic. The Black King has become the populist *Le Grand Chef* all over again; Duplessis's dealings with the

English are again seen as successful diddling rather than silent surrender; his autocracy and Red smears are perceived as the natural by-products of a tough confrontationist Quebec politician — someone perhaps like Trudeau.

The old enemy of Trudeau is now the unvarnished hero of the generations that have just followed Trudeau. Duplessis's *Deux Nations* are again alive in the hearts of the Québécois and in the minds of the Québécois trendy set. Trudeau, the Quebec single warrior, failed to exorcise Quebec's past; its future has now fallen out of his grasp. Trudeau's trials of combat have resulted in victories more Pyrrhic than Periclean, leaving behind a One Canada in which Two Solitudes have become *Deux Nations* in everything but name, a state-subsidized multiculturalism puts up one Tower of Babel after another, and a country with one of the weakest defence systems in the world is preaching the world's most self-righteous message of "Peace In Our Time."

Still, in the tricky terrain of race and creed Trudeau laid claim to some important political firsts. Trudeau was the first French Canadian prime minister to dominate the elites of both English and French Canada. St. Laurent and Laurier dominated neither. Trudeau clearly stood above Canada's intellectual and cultural elites and was certainly held in respect, if not in awe, by the business and technological elites of the country.

Trudeau was the first French Canadian prime minister to be totally relaxed and comfortable with his Frenchness. The cultural and racial apologetics of a Laurier and a St. Laurent were certainly not in the Trudeau makeup. This ethnic assertiveness and self-confidence made Trudeau the first francophone leader to openly contradict French Canada's traditional collective guilt myths. He refused to blame the wicked *anglais* or the greedy Yankee capitalists for Quebec's miseries and woes. That, Trudeau correctly blamed on Quebec's *rois nègres*, and their clerical allies who preferred the economic dotage that came with espousing the purity of their race to the economic benefits that an open competitive economy and society could give the French Canadian people. Trudeau's assertion that Quebec's history was determined by

Quebeckers and not by Bay Street or Wall Street was as responsible for Quebec's new maturity and sense of itself as were the Quiet Revolution and Expo put together.

Trudeau was the first French Canadian leader to be forgiven his conscription sins by English Canada; Laurier's were never forgotten. It was Trudeau who dealt a virtual death blow to McCarthyite politics in Canada. Red-baiting and Red-smearing had driven Einstein's biographer and colleague Leopold Infeld out of this country and diplomat Herbert Norman to suicide. Stories of Trudeau's mysterious canoe trips in Cuba and of the strange friends and colleagues that accompanied him on his first peace mission to Moscow in the '50s had their fullest circulation when Trudeau was about to come to power. Their rejection by the Canadian people in 1968 meant the official rejection of McCarthyism in Canadian politics. After Trudeau, the black arts of guilt by association and friendly witnessing could only be practised publicly by the sturdiest and most rabid of the devil's disciples.

Trudeau's airborne commando approach, the drop of the single warrior, was the order of the day as early as 1968 in the field of economic policy. Not for Plaza Pierre the slow, piecemeal gains of Walter Gordon or Mitchell Sharp. Both men were perfect Pearsonians. Gordon wished to tilt the Keynesian pendulum to buy back our industries and resources from the Americans. Sharp viewed the economy as fragile and sickly and feared American retaliation. Both men were more than eager to walk softly and carry no stick in these areas.

Not Pierre Elliott Trudeau. Like all macho men, he could not face the weak and sickly; thus Trudeau simply proclaimed our economy to be as strong and virile as he himself was and acted accordingly. A strong economy did not need Gordon's buy-back policies; a strong economy could write off the present American branch plants in the black ink of the future technologies Trudeau was sure were coming our way.

Gordon's policies were inimical to Trudeau on a more than modular basis; the economic mythologies of the two men clashed as well. Trudeau, the internationalist socialist-bureaucrat, the disciple of Elie Kadourie, Hans Kohn and Lord Acton, could see nothing but risk and peril in the espousal of economic nationalism. From this vantage point Trudeau could not help but believe that Gordon was pushing Anglo-Canadian control of the economy for his own hidden-lever purposes. Trudeau preferred the international brotherhood of capital even if the gnomes running it were the dreaded Americans; in the blind exercise of a similar rationale, Trudeau loved the Jews but was most uncomfortable with Zionism.

To Trudeau nationalism was *passé* and the future everything, especially a future spinning off new technologies every day. These technologies (for the most part American in origin and ownership) would provide Canadians with all the wealth and jobs they needed; and alas, all the deficits and unemployment they could handle too. In 1968 Trudeau laughed at the conventionalities of the old economics and trotted out for combat his Buck Rogers economic blueprints for the perfect integrated technological society. In 1984 the old Orwellian nightmares of machine-dominated man, without work and without hope, were giving a hard time to what was left of the 1968 Trudeau dream. In 1984 Horseman Pierre was presiding over still another apocalypse; gunslinger Pierre had again shot himself in one more single-warrior duel.

Not only was the Trudeau gunslinger unique to Canadian politics, but so was the American-oriented style that inevitably went with it. Certainly, from 1968 on, the Elliott in Trudeau was a Kennedyean one; the Pierre in Trudeau beat very much in rhythm with the tom-toms of a President de Gaulle and the politics of *grandeur*. (After all, both Trudeau and de Gaulle wanted bigger things for Quebec and were certainly not separatists. Trudeau wanted Quebec riveted to Canada, de Gaulle a Quebec riveted to France.)

There are no images more central to the American way than the gunslinger and the warrior-president, both mandated by the people, both dispensing justice, alone. Sometimes they are indistinguishable — Wilson and Truman versus Congress; Roosevelt versus the courts — but rarely does one find them in the Canadian context. Laurier, after all, had his Ministry of Talents (four premiers in his 1896 cabinet alone). King often lost his own seat. Uncle Louis without Uncle Howe is meaningless. Pearson's cabinet resembled a deadlocked United Nations Security Council meeting. Bennett, the Ministry of One Talent, was, of course, the singular exception to this rule.

Nor was the British pattern much different. Lloyd George was strong but not presidential. Churchill's cabinets, especially the war ones, were all-powerful.

Nor was this pattern odd. A prime minister was first among equals in the British practice because his ministers were supposed to be powerfully mandated themselves, i.e., a prime minister needed them as much as they needed him. Ministers ran their departments as much to show their followers how powerful they were as for any other reason. A resigning minister could at one time topple a government that was operating in a prime ministerial mould. When the mould turned rancid and presidential, the resignation of a powerful minister like John Turner had all the *real* effect of a marriage breakdown in Saudi Arabia.

It wasn't because Trudeau was a gifted amateur that he dealt a death blow to consensual prime ministerial politics. Pearson, St. Laurent and King (at least in 1921) were all gifted amateurs before him; King and Pearson, like Trudeau, had even had prior bureaucratic careers. Trudeau killed cabinet politics because it did not square with his peculiar Actonian sense of power. (As Trudeau himself put it: lack of power corrupts, absolute lack of power corrupts absolutely.) Trudeau could see in cabinet collegiality nothing but the pleasant smiling face of status quo politics. Trudeau's radical sensibilities were offended by the inertia of cabinet; cabinet administration meant a denial of political will, political symmetry. Certainly any man as contemptuous of past Liberal practices as Trudeau, was bound to find King's political practices and cabinet gamesmanship less than edifying.

Trudeaumania and charisma — the twin Trudeau engines driving the 1968 election campaign — were purely presidential. In

1968 the only truly successful presidential candidate on the continent was Trudeau; Canadians preferred their Trudeau-president by a golden mile to the American presidential bores — Tricky Dicky Nixon and Hube the Boob Humphrey — they contrasted him with. The 1968 election was the first in which Canadians felt that their leader was smarter, brighter, sexier than the American leader.

When a gunslinger is mandated he always brings his own boys into the O.K. Corral with him. The Trudeau PMO was thus totally presidential as well — i.e., three hundred people having the ear of a single prime minister at one and the same time, rather than the one or two sets of ears having such access in the good old days. A presidential PMO means a consolidated political power base and a body of experts to bear upon *political*, not *administrative* problems, thus vastly increasing the political clout of the presidential prime minister at the expense of his cabinet and caucus.

A presidential PMO meant a Jim Davey, an Ivan Head, a Marc Lalonde. Under Trudeau, PMO boss Lalonde became a virtual deputy prime minister. With program secretary Jim Davey, futurism, think tankism, utopian social engineering bubbled and boiled away, giving Trudeau daily a new batch of horrific ideas with which to terrify his cabinet. A presidential system like Trudeau's meant a cabinet totally unreflective of the domestic political picture. Once the Trudeau cabinet ceased to be politically relevant, Trudeau was free to scrap Mackenzie King's rules for cabinet balance and political symmetry. Trudeau could and did appoint whom he wished.

Ivan Head gave Trudeau what he always dreamt of — his very own foreign and defence policy. Head's computers moved more swiftly than the soft-shoe diplomacy of External Affairs. Thus trimming the Canadian defence establishment, while asking for a greater say in the affairs of our alliance, became not only logical but desirable in the world of Ivan Head. Gunslingers, inevitably being administrative amateurs, could not but enjoy the discomfiture all this brought to the professional diplomat and soldier.

*No true Grit—and certainly no single-combat warrior—
can escape the call of the Canadian Wild West.*

Trudeau is all smiles as Grand Marshal of the Calgary Stampede.

...d for Muriel ***B****ull Shields and Pauline White Grass.*

For a while, the Trudeau charisma ... *and*
West — certainly for the Stampede

*But the West still eludes Trudeau. Calgary has not elected
a Liberal since 1972. In 1980 from Vancouver to the
Lakehead, only two Liberals were elected—*

*and this despite the advice of the most famous Western
Liberal of them all, Alberta's Jim Coutts. Here Frère
Jacques and the Kid ponder the politics of how to stop
the Tories in the West; or maybe they're pondering the
politics of how to stop Spadina—from going anything
but Coutts.*

If the West spurned him, the solitude of the Far North offered Trudeau a home away from home.

Diefenbaker may have had his vision of the North...

. . . but Trudeau was the first prime minister to be a true northerner strong and free.

And if the lure of the North and the Last Best West failed to keep Trudeau's charisma count up, there were other masks to wear: the Codfather politics of the Maritime East..

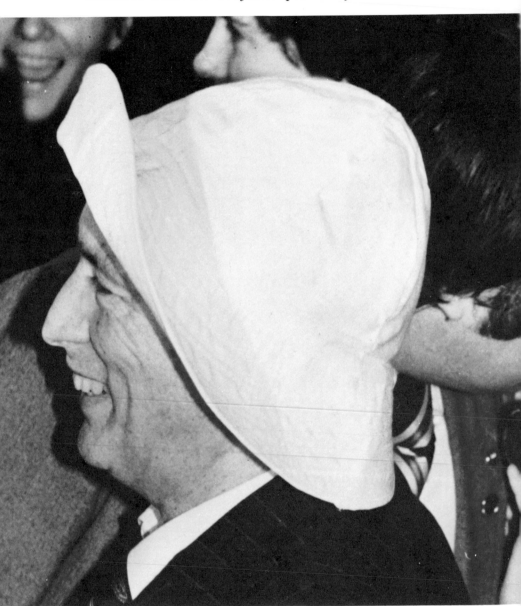

The singing paddle of the coureur de bois...

And the playful games of the native Indian.

The only problem with presidential politics is they don't reflect the realities of Canadian political life. Presidential politics mean weak cabinets; weak cabinets mean a weak democratic base; democracy poorly rooted eventually gets lopped off — at least at the head. In 1972 Trudeau campaigned as the gunslinger turned land-is-strong baron. The vulnerabilities of charisma had been replaced with the certitudes of arrogance. The president's clothes still had not been sent to the cleaners.

Trudeau's quick hustle back to parliamentary politics after 1972 indicated a lesson absorbed rather than learned. After his 1974 victory, Trudeau still itched for the hunting patterns of the lone wolf. In 1979, for the first time (repeated to some extent in 1980), Trudeau styled himself a gunslinger and on one empty stage after another defied Canadians to shoot him down.

It is ironic that 1984 should mark the rites of passage for Pierre Elliott Trudeau. Many Canadians hoped 1984 would never come; many many more never dreamt that Orwellian year would spell the end of the Trudeau epoch. Still 1984 did not bring us a Trudeau watching out for us on the Rideau with Big Brotherly Love, nor was the Prime Minister's Office broadcasting any more newspeak or doublethink than usual. Nor did 1984 really bring an end to the mad mad world of P.E.T. Certainly it's not every country whose Leader of the Opposition publicly berates a candidate for the Liberal leadership for not being, like himself, Trudeauish enough. It is passing strange but certainly Canadian, that a Leader of the Opposition would model himself, philosophically and intellectually, on a prime minister he has spent twenty years of his life opposing. It is also the best of Canadian symmetries that in 1968 Trudeau was bitterly attacked by the radical chichi and Beautiful People of anglophonia for his espousal of One Canada over the then trendy dogmas of *Deux Nations* and associate statehood; in 1984 the radical chichi and the Beautiful People were busy attacking John Turner for deviating, albeit an inch, from the now trendy Trudeau One Canada line.

By 1984 much of the Trudeau blitzkrieg of 1968 was stalled and abandoned on the highways and byways of Canada. Multiculturalism, originally intended as a sop to Canadian ethnics, automatically made second class by bilingualism and biculturalism, had by 1984 become a trivializing wasteful lottery; the only winners in this game being ethnic association presidents and ethnic newspaper editors whose supposed representation of their fellow ethnics won them free-flowing government grants to keep themselves and their brethren ethnically intact. Bilingualism, the supposed twinning of the tongues of Canada, had become a virtual blank cheque for the hiring and promotion of the super elites of Anglo-Saxon and French Canada. In this 1984 Trudeau world, race and creed are more important than ever before; the peevish bigotries of Mackenzie King certainly pale before the realities of a 1984 Trudeau world where integration, interaction and assimilation are bad words for bad ideas and where opportunities for the top jobs in the country are virtually denied to ninety-nine per cent of the population.

Trudeau's my-way politics had always involved, perhaps accidentally, the shutting out, the barring, the punishing of large numbers of people. Trudeau's language and constitution politics bitterly isolated the Canadian WASP, particularly the WASPs of small-town and rural Canada. With no room for Babbitt in Trudeau's Camelot, Babbitt found murkier and more nativist waters to splash around in. In 1972 the WASP Canada that had cheered itself blue, deaf and dumb on War Measures, gave its collective thumbs down to Trudeau; in 1979 WASP Canadians did so again; in 1984 these same WASP Canadians barred Trudeau's re-entry into political orbit.

The politics of doing it my way meant a Trudeau coalition of French Canadians and ethnics, that by 1984 could not keep on winning because the basic population element of the country bitterly opposed it. WASP Canada may have fallen out of love with Trudeau, but Trudeau, alas, had never really given it more than a fleeting acknowledgment of his unrequited indifference to their pervasive fallibility.

My-way politics were also reflected in the Trudeau samurai skin-deep sensitivity to the organized bastions of criticism. The

Acton countervailer, the *Cité libre* critic, the pen-wielding swordsman of repartee and dialectic wit seemingly did not relish the more prosaic gunslingers of Trudeauphobia. *Les affaires* fuddle duddle and *mange la merde* symbolically revealed Trudeau in a far less charitable mood towards criticism than his Sun King status would have implied. Referring to opposition MPs as ''nobodies'' was natural to a Trudeau who in 1963 viewed Liberal MPs as sheep; but in Trudeauland, if both the MPs who criticized him and the MPs who slavishly followed him were weak, so were Trudeau's cabinets, which rarely dared to criticize or withstand him. This left Trudeau and the Prime Minister's Office as the only ones worthy of the respect and affection — of Trudeau and the Prime Minister's Office.

Certainly the fourth estate was conspicuously absent from Trudeau's Camelot once it had served its purpose of whipping up and then dispensing the twin tablets of charisma and Trudeaumania. Trudeau's dislike of the press and of WASP Canada were really two sides of the same coin. The press was loaded with more than its share of the yahoos, Babbitts, bores and bigot unilinguals of English Canada. Trudeau's rejection of the press was once again the affirmation of the superiority of his own my-way politics.

The 1984 fall of Trudeau was as inevitable as the 1968 rise. In 1968, Trudeau was the darling of the press, of English Canada, of the upwardly mobile ethnics, of French Canada, of women, kids and dogs. In 1984, Trudeau, desperately clinging to the Camelot ideals, frantically stormed the most important bastions of the world to bring *them* a peace he could not bring to his own people. World leaders do not jump out of their own frying pans into the domestic frying pans of others that easily. Had Trudeau been more successful at home, he would have been more successful abroad. The Trudeau Peace Mission, and Trudeau's almost desperate desire to cling to office, were the last-gasp politics of doing it my way. Both had to work simultaneously or not at all.

In 1984 Trudeau was certainly prepared to serve once more, if only the Liberal troops and the public would fall discreetly and obediently into place behind him. In 1984 the Trudeau bugles called but no one came, and no one stayed for dinner. In 1984 the coalition of 1968 had gone its own way. In 1984 Trudeau, Canada's only Olympian Living Political God, watched the idolators successfully invade his temple.

In 1984 Trudeau scored one of the most embarrassing firsts in Canadian history: he became the first prime minister to be driven from office by public opinion before an election. Diefenbaker's purgatory occurred after his last prime ministerial election; the hated Bennett was driven out only in the 1935 election; Arthur Meighen and St. Laurent left voluntarily after election defeats; Pearson departed quietly while still at relative peace with public opinion; Laurier died in harness as a reigning Liberal leader.

Still there is much to be said about my-way politics. The Trudeau legislative accomplishment is truly remarkable. Trudeau's personal greatness has made all Canadians a little bit greater. French Canada's rightful place in Confederation was restored by Trudeau; Canadian ethnics may be second class, but under Trudeau they are the most resourceful and best-off ethnics in the world. The Trudeau coalition of 1968 will someday be picked up by other hands.

The politics of my way are gone forever; 1984 will surely pass; but one thing is certain: Pierre Elliott Trudeau in fact and in myth is here to stay — in the minds and hearts of most Canadians. Trudeau's my way will remain one journey they were glad they made — or never made.

The Trudeau years, 1968-1984, are more than a watershed in Canadian life; they are a powerful beginning in search for a meaningful end — or perhaps the Trudeau years are simply a powerful beginning to what, by 1984, had become a mindless, meaningless end game.

2 The Sexual Combat of the Single Warrior

The Turks have their delights, the English their titles, but Canada has its national fires perpetually stoked with the purest of piggy ironies. To the rest of the world the Dionne quintuplets were a miracle; but the Canadian sense of irony demanded that to Anglo-Saxon Canada the quintuplets were proof that the French revenge of the cradle now had a new secret weapon, the Gatling Gun of mass conception. Certainly every self-respecting Canadian irony monger knows that Canada is the only country to have hosted two of history's most important conferences — the Quebec conferences of 1942 and 1944 — without being invited to either one. And Canada is the one country where a head of state got most of his advice from the dead, advice that always proved right — dead right, so to speak.

But what could be more Canadian and ironic than the anointing, in the year of Our Lord 1968, of a shy, short, introverted, Jesuit-trained, single-combat warrior Québécois as Canada's biggest sex symbol since Barbara Ann Scott? Did Trudeau deserve this transferred sexual exaltation? Did the women (and gay men) whose sexual transport for Trudeau was so extensive that it could only be shipped by sea in supertankers, misread him or misread themselves? Or both? Did the single-combat warrior ever worry about women making sex a two-combat affair? How did this positive recluse take to the sexual droolings of his new-found fans? Did Mr. Reason Above Passion reason correctly that in politics, passion always transcends reason and provides the only power base that reason can act upon successfully in the first place?

Did Trudeau ever really know what charisma and its sexual overtones meant? Was the poisoned chalice of charisma passed to his lips by the media or was that sacrament passed on in the reverse direction? Did the middle-aged lady running open-armed across the Yellowknife airport tarmac to hug and kiss Trudeau simply love the leader of our country to distraction, or was Trudeau the closest thing to a movie star offering sublimated sex, freely obtained and painlessly enjoyed, that the Northwest Territories had ever seen?

The answers to these questions will probably have to await Trudeau's memoirs — which he has often assured the nation will never be written. In the meantime, perhaps Freudian analysis, if kept in proportion, can shed some light on Trudeau's charisma. Such an assessment excludes, of course, the simplistic Freudian observations the amateur psychologist quickly makes about Trudeau — such as his losing his father at an early age and being too close to his mother ever since. What is important about Trudeau is not his obvious Freudian flowchart; rather it is the fact that he is the first prime minister in Canadian history to practise and preach the politics of sex.

Under Justice Minister Trudeau, homosexual rights and easy divorce were debated for the first time. So was abortion and the right to life. These issues got the state out of the bedrooms of the nation; and they got Pierre Elliott Trudeau into the drawing rooms and living rooms of the elites of English Canada. This major foray into sexual politics won Trudeau the leadership of the Liberal Party. Charisma, the ultimate orgiastic celebration of sexual politics, won Trudeau his biggest and only truly national majority victory. Without the politics of sex, there never would have been Trudeau the prime minister, Trudeau the Man of War Measures and Trudeau the world peace missionary.

The joys of Trudeau charisma brought to Canadian politics in 1968 what John and Bob Kennedy had already brought to Yankee politics. But in the Dominion of the North, this Kennedy sex appeal was bested by Trudeau's sexual suzerainty. As a sex symbol for Canadians, John Kennedy married to the exquisite Jacqueline was no match for our own red-rose Pierre, bachelor extraordinaire. As for Bobby and his cheaper-by-the-dozen family, his sex appeal was strictly intra-mural and his appeal more demagogic than charismatic. Politics and sex, it seems, was obviously an even more potent mix in Trudeau Canada than in Fortress America.

Charisma denotes, above all, sublimated sex. The charismatic politician, simply put, gets you off, without your having to do anything active about it. Being a great orator, or a great crowd pleaser, has nothing to do with charisma. Diefenbaker was a fantastic crowd pleaser and orator but certainly not charismatic; no one took cold showers after listening to Diefenbaker's Vision of the North.

The closest thing to sex in Canadian politics before Trudeau was "the dirty old man" syndrome artfully pursued by Mackenzie King and improved upon by his successor. Mackenzie King just loved the presence on his lap of famous pretty little girls — Shirley Temple, the Dionne quintuplets, and his all-time favourite, Barbara Ann Scott. All these lovely young things Mackenzie King would reward with a fatherly, lust-sublimated peck on each of their extended cheeks. No child molester anywhere could have ever had more fun than old "Rex" King with his starlets. Wisely, official photographers always recorded these happy events for use as Mackenzie King propaganda in up-and-coming elections.

This slight foray into sexual politics by King was taken into overdrive by St. Laurent. On the campaign trail, St. Laurent kissed everything that moved. Lovely little girls also sat on his lap while Uncle Louie played with the Shawinigan mugs and Minnedosa doilies they had brought as expressions of their home-town civic virtue. The Québécois emptied their cradles for him. Child shelters and orphanages from Fortune, Newfoundland to Terrace, British Columbia opened their doors to St. Laurent's pursed lips. The grand old man from the Grand Allée, dared to kiss male Québécois by the dozen, and got away with it. All this osculation too had Freudian overtones to it, but the stream of unconscious votes it poured into the ballot box also turned St. Laurent, a most unsexy and uncharismatic man, into the sexless castrate caricature known as Uncle Louis.

But all this King-St. Laurent kiss-and-show oscillation was mere flirtation, mere Harlequin Romance, compared to the grand passion of Trudeau charisma. Certainly power may have had something to do with Trudeau charisma. Power may tend to corrupt but it also tends to arouse curiosity and passion, and where these two are, sex is not far behind.

Trudeau, once in power, began to generate exotic and passionate tales unlike any other prime minister in Canadian history. Mackenzie King would certainly not have wandered around in a burnoose and knapsack on the sands of Arabia. The diplomat Pearson would not have been mistaken as an Israeli spy and incarcerated by the Jordanian police. R. B. Bennett, enemy of the people, would never have thrown a snowball at Stalin's statue in Moscow. None of these men would have joined Trudeau in a trip to Peking, the Forbidden Red City of godless China, at the very height of McCarthyism.

Like Inspector Clouseau, our Trudeau was prepared to karate-chop into oblivion the hated separatists of Quebec; Trudeau might not have always succeeded, but he was the first brown belt to be prime minister. Trudeau was the first prime minister to shoot the rapids of the Coppermine River. Trudeau was the first prime minister to climb the nearest mountain at the drop of a Tyrolean hat. And the first prime minister to be photographed diving into a swimming pool was named Pierre Elliott Trudeau. Physically and athletically Trudeau made the bully-bully Teddy Roosevelt seem a mere thick-spectacled myopic. By the Trudeau standard, Johnson, Nixon and Humphrey looked like Larry, Curly and Moe.

Trudeau's charisma was thus quite explainable. In 1968 an insecure nation had just finished celebrating its real independence, the world recognition that came with Expo. Trudeau was our permanent Expo; as long as we had him, Canada could warrior-

Mens sana, in sano corpore —

the healthy mind in the beautiful body is the basic credo of a charismatic leader. It is equally a staple of the politics of sex.

Trudeau shakes the pelvis of his Body Beautiful, like no other sixty-year-old prime minister has ever done before.

It's the night of the hunter and Trudeau takes a mighty bow and bends it.

It's the old man and the sea: Trudeau is our first surfing prime minister.

The first prime minister to be photographed diving into a pool.

The first prime minister to bounce on a trampoline.

The first prime minister to fly a jet.

The first prime ministerial hustler.

The first prime minister to dance sheik to sheik.

combat with anyone and any country. Trudeau's spiritual powers, his athletic prowess, his intellectual class, his sex appeal, made him our permanent and only superstar. With more charisma and sexual ooomph than any leader in the world, Canada just had to love Pierre Trudeau. And where there's love, there's sex. Where there's sex, there's the politics of sex and Trudeau was Canada's first practitioner of that new gift of the magi.

Not everyone joined Trudeau in the politics of sex, and some loved him more truly than others. None loved him more intensely than the homosexuals he liberated legislatively in 1968. The gays found Trudeau attractive, both politically and sexually. By taking the state out of the bedrooms of the nation, Trudeau had become the Third Man for the Third Sex. The gay vote became Trudeau's exclusive preserve.

In 1968 gay votes affected few, if any, seats, but just as the bigots who hated Trudeau believed he was gay (after all, he was the Lincoln of the gays), the gays too believed that Trudeau was bi and bi sexually. The gay view simply reinforced the bigot view of Trudeau. Together the bigots and gays were part of a sexual politics that was revolutionary in Canada. For the first time sexual deviation was an issue on the Canadian political scene, and a new twist on Trudeau's politics of sex was accidentally born.

The Trudeau charisma affected heterosexual men quite differently. Watching the effect Trudeau was having on Canadian women, heterosexual men came to one of two conclusions. Those unsure of their masculinity, intimidated by the new feminist or sex manual heresies, were equally intimidated by Trudeau, whose obvious sexual prowess made them feel they possessed none. These men sought out Stanfield, the kind of man whose sexual charisma gifts they could accept, and did not envy.

The urbane sophisticated straight Canadian males saw in Trudeau charisma pure vicarious sexual atonement. Pierre was turning on women they wanted to turn on and was doing things in the bedrooms of the nation they knew they could do if only given a chance. In the field of sex Pierre allowed them the grandstand quarterbacking privileges they already had with Saturday afternoon football on TV.

When Pierre went after the earthy and explicit Eva Rittenhaus, Canada's sexual grandstand quarterbacks knew for certain they could make that off-tackle play too. When Pierre dated the beauteous Jennifer Rae, a classy diplomat's daughter, oozing sex appeal from every porcelain pore in her body, Canada's sexual grandstand quarterbacks knew they could *not* make *that* play.

Canada's swingers liked Pierre because his sexual politics were the best spectator sport in the country. To them Pierre was as straight as an arrow. They saw Trudeau not as a homosexual, but in the old-fashioned sense of the word, as the gayest of gay blades. Politically and sexually he was their kind of guy, and in 1968 Canada's swingers gave Trudeau their vote. When in 1972 Trudeau deliberately killed the politics of charisma with his marriage and his assumption of the new role of super manager-bureaucrat, Canada's swingers were the first set of voters to abandon him.

Bourgeois French women in Canada were more immune to Trudeau's sexy stuff than their sisters in anglophonia. Sophisticated female Quebec already knew Pierre, from thousands of previous social and personal contacts. Pierre was a nice French boy who took out nice French girls — like the academic beauty Madeleine Gobeil and the gorgeous actress Louise Marleau. He had all the charisma and sex appeal of an altar boy. To these Quebec women Pierre was a socialist, a feminist, a good Catholic and a good Liberal. They voted for him out of reason, not passion.

While Trudeau's sexual politics was a minimal factor with Quebec women, Québécois men lacked anglophonia's grandstand quarterback culture and so voted for Pierre because he was a good Liberal. Trudeau was good for their sense of peoplehood; he did nothing for their libidos.

Trudeau's sexual politics also scored with the rich and sophisticated women and men of Toronto's Rosedale and Forest Hill, Montreal's Mount Royal and Westmount, Vancouver's Shaughnessy Heights, Calgary's Eagle Ridge, Edmonton's Crestwood and Winnipeg's River Heights. In these Canadian fiefdoms of upper-middle-class wealth and glamour, the clang of chastity belts dropping on the floor could be heard for miles when Plaza Pierre was in town.

To these anglophone women Pierre was more than pure sex, he was also pure exotica. They looked on Trudeau in the same way as rich women once looked lasciviously on the exotic Jack Johnson, the first black heavyweight champion of the world. Before Trudeau they were too well bred to openly admit that Quebec was exotic, alien, forbidden, sexy. In 1968, with Trudeau's charismatic politics, Canada's anglophone female aristocracy treated Trudeau and Quebec as mysterious exotics, and no one in Canada accused them either of condescension or chauvinism. These superior, snobbish, rich anglophone ladies who had once laughed at the primitive *habitants* were now saying the French were sexier, brighter and tougher than anglophones; why shouldn't they run the country?

Trudeau's sexual politics carried away the Beautiful People — the Hadassah bazaarniks and the Junior Leaguers, the York and Petroleum Clubbers. It was also the Beautiful People who in 1968 won for Trudeau the rich upper-class seats of the Canadian West.

Trudeau also carried a very important subspecies of the Beautiful People — their radical chichi brothers and sisters of the media-intellectual set. John Gray and his beautiful and talented wife Elizabeth were buying Trudeau holus-bolus in 1968. So were the Rotsteins, the Frums, Jack and Barbara McLeod, the Ramsay Cooks, the Saywells, the Adrienne and Stephen Clarksons, the Patrick Watsons, the Hurtigs, and Peter and Christina Newman.

To these people the orgiastic aspects of Trudeau's sexual politics were irrelevant. What was relevant was the substantive part of that sexual politics — reforms on abortion, divorce and gay rights. To the Thinking People these were proof enough of Trudeau's Liberalism.

To the hard-core feminists, Trudeau's sexual reforms were not quite enough; nor was the fact that he was the first male champion of female causes enough to detach many feminist votes from the NDP. But enough feminists *did* go to Trudeau to make this an interesting sidebar to the politics of sex. These feminists knew that Trudeau's reforms would legitimize their movement; Trudeau had seen their future and made them realize it would work. Feminist militancy in Canada did not precede Trudeau, it followed him. Still, 1968 was the last time the radical chichi would give mass support to Trudeau. War Measures, and refusal by Trudeau to push abortion on demand and adequate day-care, were enough to keep the Feminist Freedom Fighters on the other side of the Trudeau barricades.

But Trudeau's politics of sex grew even more unusual fauna than the radical chichi. In 1968 even the ordinary wives of ordinary workers were going gaga for Trudeau. To these working-class women, Trudeau was not an embodiment of French versus English, but the first sexy movie-star politician they had run across, in the flesh, in their drab working-class lives. These proletarian women went for Trudeau in droves, cancelling out their husbands' NDP votes and threatening total oblivion for Canada's only surviving democratic socialist party. The Trudeau politics of sex, it seemed, had performed Canadian political miracles — it transcended all three sexual divisions and all social and economic classes in Canada. Trudeau's charisma had made Canada One.

But Trudeau's politics of sex had its dangerous side too. For one thing its pace could not be kept up; and in 1972 charisma was dropped, and Trudeau nearly dropped along with it. By 1972 Trudeau the sexual mystery man was a frog happily married to an Anglo-Saxon princess; in 1972 Trudeau was the super-straight chief executive officer of State Canada.

Marriage kills charisma as quickly and as effectively as the neutron bomb kills everyone. The married Trudeau, in Hollywood parlance, had kissed away his political box-office for a mess of matrimonial dotage. Besides, it was not a well kept secret that Pierre was no longer amused by the passion politics of sex. In 1972 he decided to run on the bright pure reason of bureaucratic excellence. Trudeau told the press he was the best business manager in the country and that his cabinet was the best management team in Canada. In the campaign, Trudeau's second greatest political disaster, not a gasp, squeal or giggle could be heard in the land; charisma was out, and business-as-usual was the political staple of Trudeau's garrison mentality.

It was equally true that sexual politics could not withstand true crises like War Measures. Once Trudeau became Napoleon in October 1970, he could hardly again revert to the Hollywood sex symbol of old; no more than President Reagan can ever again become the Voice of the Turtle. Finally, as inevitable as was the demise of Trudeau's sexual politics, so too was the inevitability that it would have a dark, down side. That dark, down side was a nasty marriage breakdown, the real or Margaret-fancied cuckolding of the prime minister, the bitterness, frustration and public humiliation of Trudeau — a confluence of circumstances that forever ruled out the playful pyrotechnics of charisma politics for P.E.T.

Trudeau's sexual politics also had a political down side that few of the Trudeaumaniacs and Beautiful People of 1968 would have thought possible. Despite Trudeau's physical and athletic prowess and obvious courage, despite the beauties forever draped on his arm, despite the two Christmas babies and three sons, Trudeau's politics of sex had for a sizable proportion of the country posed the question: how manly was Trudeau's manliness? The doubts first surfaced among the right-wing element of the Tory caucus — the very element most opposed to Trudeau's alleged Frenchification of the country.

These Tory doubts were spread rapidly to their constituents. In 1968 this Tory bigot vote concluded that Trudeau the brown belt, canoeist and mountain climber always climbed into bed with the wrong sex. These haters of the French fact did not view all francophones as faggots; they hated Marc Lalonde but never doubted his sexuality, nor Chrétien's, nor that of a Romeo like Leblanc. But now they could and did argue that bilingualism was a Trudeau ploy and, therefore, a homosexual ploy, and as good Moral Majoritarians they could reassure themselves that their opposition to Trudeau on bilingualism was sexual, not racist.

Didn't Trudeau make abortion legal and divorce easier? Were not these aberrations the twin pillars of the devil, out to destroy the Christian family? Who, if not homosexuals, were the biggest enemies of the Christian family? These were the questions the Tory bigots asked themselves. The Tory bigot vote, now marshalled against Trudeau, felt certain that they avoided the stigma of bigotry in all this. A racial crusade, they felt, could now be safely turned into a religious crusade. As good religious fundamentalist folks, the Canadian Tory bigot vote could now say St. Laurent was an okay Frenchman but a Sodomite like Trudeau went beyond the pale.

Soon the Moral Majority freaks came up with a new and quite peculiar scenario — namely the civil servant as sex object in Trudeau's politics of sex. Despite the fact that the Clerk of the Privy Council, Michael Pitfield, had all the sex appeal of Mr. Dressup, Tory bigots and Moral Majoritarians insisted that nightlong sessions in the PMO between Pitfield and Trudeau were more a carnival in Rideau than consensus in Consecon.

For this scenario there was also confirmation in the strangest places. The yahoos were not the only ones to get gulled by the Pitfield-Trudeau garbage; Liberals and reformers, perhaps of the Pearson or NDP stripe, frightened of Trudeau personally and of their places in the sun around him supported this theory too. At Rockcliffe parties and over lunch, they told the Jaded Observer off-colour jokes about the Ottawa Sun God, jokes that always fanned the fires of Trudeau's alleged homosexuality. Soon much of the media, in private, was at play on the same turf and at the same game.

Now the Tory bigots could also get indirect media confirmation for their Sodomite scenario by simply reading between the lines of sex-obsessed Fifth Columns of respectable, even radical, columnists and newspapermen. Should this not prove satisfactory, the yahoo-Tory wing could get the benediction of Canada's French Fifth Column; Trudeau's own racial compatriots, the separatists, and their sympathizers, were always willing to bear false witness to Trudeau's alleged moral turpitudes.

In the politics of sex, the charismatic leader must establish a princely penchant for beautiful princesses.

The prince who is in the constant company of beautiful women such as Quebec actress Denise Filatrault establishes clearly that both his masculinity and inner spirituality are irresistible even to goddesses.

When the prince squires such a princess he tells one and all that he is the only true prince...

*. . . and by following and worshipping him, all in the land
are made wiser, more beautiful, more charismatic.*

With Trudeau on a social occasion early in 1968 was Jennifer Rae, an active media worker in his leadership campaign.

Ms Rae encapsulated in one person the multi-communication modes that catapulted Trudeau to power. Jennifer's father, Saul Rae, was one of Canada's most distinguished diplomats; he was also co-author with pollster Dr. George Gallup of a book on communications theory. Saul's brother, Jackie, was one of the CBC's early variety stars. Jennifer's brother, Bob, is the leader of the Ontario NDP; another brother, Johnny, was Jean Chrétien's leadership campaign manager. Jennifer is married to Bruce Yaccatto, a CTV reporter.

In the politics of sex, there is only a classless society.

The good socialist politician who knows beauty is neither skin- nor class-deep also rewards the beauties of the working class. Trendy Trudeau deftly autographs the blouse of St. Catharines waitress Helen Turner.

In the rear view mirror of Trudeau charisma, pert, handsome blondes prefer gentlemen. The preferring blonde — Globe and Mail *reporter Debbie Monk.*

This is Trudeau charisma at its best and the politics of sex at its most potent.

The Trudeau potion always worked best with older women; they found in him raptures of joy and spiritual fulfilment that their more prosaic husbands or boy-friends had long ago ceased providing.

But what is truly stunning here is that this woman so rapturously greeting Trudeau is matched in her enthusiasm by a new kind of political leader — one whose genuine joy in people, at least in the heady days of 1968, was rivalled by few politicians anywhere in the world.

Here then is charisma in a chalice, a sexual communion in which neither the prime minister nor his female constituent get the short end of the stick.

Should the charismatic leader tire of the politics of sex and wish to put an end to them, then he must take unto himself a young and beautiful princess.

Her youth should restore him, her beauty quicken him, her worship increase the self-love the charismatic one needs to function.

But should the princess begin to tire of her liege, then it's best for everyone if the charismatic leader...

. . . simply lets her go.

But for the Tory yahoos the best confirmation for Trudeau's supposed perversions came from the Tory yahoos' own philosopher king, Ron Gostick of Flesherton, Ontario. Gostick, incidentally, published the *Canadian Intelligence Service*, the Canadian anti-Semite's best guide for Jew watching-hating-boycotting-and-bashing.

Gostick, now seeing Trudeau as Jewish, naturally became Canada's leading Trudeauphobe; as such, his pamphlets voraciously peddled the Trudeau as Semite-Sodomite line. These pamphlets were already in mass circulation in 1968 in places as far away as Newfoundland. At lunch with Premier Smallwood and Senator Paul Martin, the Jaded Observer was told by the last Father of Confederation that Gostick's pamphlets had killed Trudeau in Newfoundland in 1968.

Gostick was certainly no Newfie joke. If the Newfs could buy his bile, why couldn't simple red-neck Tories and sex-starved Moral Majoritarians believe that Trudeau, always drenched in female beauty, really lusted after the beast Pitfield and the insouciant bachelors Sunny Al MacEachen and Kootchie-Koo Coutts?

These obscenities were really in and of themselves one of the great ironies of Canadian political history. Certainly they were the greatest irony of Trudeau's politics of sex. To the really simple folk who populated Canada's suburban Scarborough deserts and their semi-arid rural holdings, empty vessels always made the loudest noise. The loudest noises being made by anyone in Trudeau's charisma politics of sex was Trudeau. Hence his vessel of sex, heterosexually speaking, was the emptiest.

Nor did this rural-urban racist peasantry see anything unusual in Gostick's attacks on Trudeau, even though they were a Canadian first. Gostick's stuff differed quite markedly from the normal French-English, Catholic-Protestant prejudices that were the staples of Canadian politics. With Gostick the red-necks simply moved from the normal yahoo Tory *canard* that communism is Liberalism and Jewish, to Liberalism is young and *gay*.

This new dimension of the politics of sex, pushed by Canadian fascists and bought by the Tory ultra right, brought fascist preoccupation with sexual perversion to the Canadian political scene for the first time. This twist worked even in Quebec. There the FLQ peddled the line that Trudeau was a *tapette*, a homosexual. Not only in Newfoundland but in the small towns of the West and rural Ontario, and in the taverns of east end Montreal, Trudeau's alleged deviation was taken for granted.

All this sexual McCarthyism is brand new to Canadian politics. No other prime minister's sexuality, not even Mackenzie King's, was ever called into question. Nor did Canadians ever mind studs, be they Sir John A. or Laurier. The perception, still current among many Canadians, of Trudeau as a homosexual, is a novel prejudice in Canadian politics. This kind of first Trudeau certainly did not count on when he launched his charisma politics of sex. One thing is safe to say: Trudeau was our first prime minister ever to be crucified by sexual McCarthyism. Trudeau will not be the last.

3 More Elliott than Trudeau?

"He's more Elliott than Trudeau" was a derisive phrase the Jaded Observer first heard bandied about in the Ottawa Gallery by one John Gray. (When this bone mot of contention was first dropped like a burning feather on the Jaded Observer's fevered crotch, he found it a bit puzzling. Did Gray mean that John was more Galbraith than Kenneth? Vita Sackville more East than West? And Banting better than Best? To the Jaded Observer all this was casuistry; to him the sum of the parts was always better than the parting of the sums.)

John Gray is the son of a Rosedale-bred, distinguished, Brahmin publisher and is in his own right one of Ottawa's most balanced and astute reporters. Gray's salon socialism had convinced him that Trudeau was selling his people out — of Confederation — while René Lévesque was really selling them in. The Jaded Observer had always assumed vice versa and was intrigued by Gray's thesis; it, like Gray's Elegy, had only one funereal postulate: Trudeau was really an Anglo-Saxon like his half-Scottish Elliott mother. As such, Trudeau really understood only English Canada and not the ameliorative spa cures of French Canadian nationalism. In this radical chichi thesis, being an English Canadian Elliott, Trudeau could no more help War Measures and other betrayals of the French than Wolfe could have grounded the Plains of Abraham.

To Gray and his fellow Rosedale radicals, Trudeau was a cynical *vendu* selling out his own Québécois people (who, according

29

to Gray, were oddly enough not Trudeau's own people) to the *maudits anglais* (who oddly enough really were Trudeau's own people). So in the Gray thesis, Trudeau was far more a slaver than a *vendu*: since he was not really French at all, he was not even selling out his *own* people.

But the real problem with Trudeau was that he was not Elliott *enough*. Neither Trudeau nor his part-Scottish mother understood any of English Canada's real rhythms. Trudeau, for example, was not anti-monarchy or anti-British; in his gut he understood neither the institutions of monarchy nor the English Canadian country that most cherished it; therefore, he simply did not understand English Canada's lust for the British connection. English Canadians (to Trudeau a "weak-kneed bleeding heart" lot) needed a sense of Britishness to make them feel important and superior to the damn Yankees.

But this insight Trudeau did not fully grasp. Nor could Frog Trudeau really turn on to the magic the Welsh prince and his Lady Di had for English Canadians; nor could he ever understand the English CBC's love for the BBC or the University of Toronto's slavish preoccupation with Oxford and Cambridge. Nor did the Outremont Outrider, dressed in a German uniform driving his motorcycle through wartime English Montreal, ever understand English Canada's desperate desire to be as class-ridden as Britain, and kept in its proper place in an Empire upon whose shores the sun was already setting at least a thousand times a day.

Trudeau, far less Elliott than Trudeau, was much more reluctant to touch the British connection than either Pearson or King. King never did touch the British connection in stylistic emotional terms, only in substance. Being always the perfect filet of mole, King's subterranean evasiveness with British imperialists won for us the right to sign our own treaties (the first, naturally enough, was on fish) and the power to have British governors-general like Vimy Ridge Byng go over the top strictly on the civilian non-combatant advice of Canadian prime ministers. The declaration of war became our natural right because of Mackenzie King. It was the diplomat Pearson who went after the formality of the British connection; instead of the pageantry of British history on our flag, scoutmaster Lester went nature trail a-blazin' and gave us a leaf to cloak our civic nakedness and a maple to hang our national pride on.

Before the appearance of the constitution question and its answer, The Canada Act, Trudeau's Brit-bashing was mild, almost illusory by comparison. True, he removed the Royal Coat of Arms from government cheques and tried to take the Royal out of the RCMP, Centre Block washrooms and the parliamentary restaurant, but he did leave the Speaker with the Mace and his old Black Rod in place.

Nor was Brit-bashing on his mind when Trudeau unravelled the longest, most meaningful and most civil libertarian constitution since the adoption of the Soviet Constitution of 1934. Trudeau the rationalist only sought a more symmetrical federalism, a new confederation to which he could play Father; he was certainly not seeking any diminution in the almost slavish affection Canadians had for the Royal Family, its weddings and trappings.

After all, Trudeau had nothing against Anglo-Saxons or Celts. His mother was half-Scottish, the mother of his children was Anglo-Saxon and with the exception of temporary romances with French, Irish and Jewish actresses and a longer one with a French intellectual, Trudeau's ladyloves from Toronto to Texas were the trendiest of WASPs.

Pro-Anglo-Saxon feelings were also strong at the Trudeau ancestral home. Papa was a Quebec Conservative à la Pierre Sévigny. The successful among the conquered of Quebec were always quick to admire the conquerors, for it was under the conquerors that they prospered. Quebec Tories, French and English, were always more pro-monarchy and pro-conscription than the Queen or King. Had Papa Trudeau lived, Pierre would certainly have served in World War II. In any event, Pierre interpreted conscription only in pure imperialist terms; his muted love of English ways was not affected by his emotional anti-conscription activities.

When to Trudeau's surprise his constitution brought on a huge

Anglo-Saxon and British Canadian backlash, then and only then was he prepared to play the biggest Brit-basher in Canadian history. He rallied Canadian ethnics and the Québécois around him. Even the Trudeauphobic Canadian press, always nationalistic, stepped in to fight their Fleet Street brethren, editorial for editorial, thinkpiece for thinkpiece.

Trudeau told the British Parliament to pass his constitution or face a British North American Ian Smith declaring unilaterial independence in two official languages and one hundred multicultural ones. When the British came to woo Canadian public opinion and found they were talking to Tory WASP Canada alone, Trudeau attacked these British envoys as if they were trying to carve up Canada just as the Halifax-Chamberlain peace mission carved up Czechoslovakia. The Brits were bashed and not appeased and Prime Minister Thatcher was abashed and Pierre-plexed. When the smoke lifted, many Canadian Anglo-Saxons were not happy with the constitution. Unhappily for them, they were only thirty-four per cent of the population, and the French and the ethnics that wanted a Canadian rather than another British North American constitution held the trump cards.

Trudeau's tattered triumph hurt Canadian national unity even more than Pearson did and certainly more than Mackenzie King. But Trudeau's constitutional way was really not anti-British or anti-Anglo-Saxon, any more than War Measures was anti-French or pro-British Canadian. Once again Trudeau was more substantive in his fight against the British connection than Pearson was with his flag and King with his semantic shtick of replacing bad British words like Imperial Federation with good Canadian ones like Halibut Treaty, bad Imperial slogans like "ready, eh, ready" with better Canadian ones — like "conscription if necessary but not necessarily conscription."

Trudeau did hurt the British connection, but luckily because of Trudeauphobia the Canadian English could only hate Trudeau and not blame the Québécois for it or fan the anti-French flames. The constitution wounds would heal but Trudeau's reputation as Canada's biggest Brit-basher would remain forever intact.

For students of esoterica it is worth noting that Trudeau is also the most successful Brit-basher in French Canadian history. Laurier had the very modesty of a prioress when it came to pulling at the unicorn. His all-Canadian navy, supposedly autonomous, promised in the event of war to provide the first Empire ships in enemy waters. In 1911 Laurier's navy sunk Laurier; his British-bashing was not a knockout blow but merely the annoying tickle of a denuded feather.

There was more in the way of feathers when conscription came along in 1917. Had Sir Wilfrid chosen to, he could have raised the fleur-de-lis and the racial blood cry of "maîtres chez nous," and pulled Quebec out of the war. The price for that would have been trenches at home as well as in France. Laurier's gallant defence of his people and his Empire, and his rejection of conscription, the anathema of his people, saved not sundered the British connection in Canada. Laurier is really more a British hero than a French one.

St. Laurent entered King's cabinet with a promise to sell conscription to his people. He did, successfully, and thus sold himself to Mackenzie King as the anointed successor. A grateful English Canada gave St. Laurent two huge national victories. In English Canada St. Laurent was called Uncle Louis; in Quebec the names he was called were closer to Uncle Tom.

In the Boer War Uncle Tom St. Laurent rooted for the British while his classmates cheered on the Brit-bashing Boers. Uncle Louis's only contribution to Brit-bashing was to remove appeals to the British Judicial Committee of the Privy Council. Still, despite telling superpower Britain to get out of Suez and getting pushed out of office by Diefenbaker for doing so, Uncle Louis St. Laurent had not really poured lava on Canada's British connection.

But Trudeau knew that the Canadian connection can only work if the links of the British one are removed one by one. For British Canadians it was a hard thing to swallow, that their last chosen (by Trudeau) anglophone governor-general was not called something like Lord Byng of Vimy Ridge, the Marquis of Lorne or

Lord Tweedsmuir; nor did he have a good Canadian name like Vincent Massey and Roland Michener. No, this Trudeau governor-general ate perogies, spoke fourteen Slavic dialects, could dance a kazatska, was a socialist, and a winning one to boot.

The Schreyer appointment strained the British connection in Canada as much or more than the constitution. What Trudeau did with bilingualism in the armed forces made it worse. The armed forces were always the favourite toys of British Canadian males; Canadian Legion halls were their favourite watering holes.

After Pearson and Hellyer had ripped all the Britophile badges off the uniforms of the Canadian troops and forced them into one big Jello vat of unification, Trudeau came along and added further humiliation. Given bilingualism demands, most of the plum officer posts went to French Canadians. Or so the bigots reminded one and all, and added that the army was now in the hands of those who deserted or resisted conscription in droves during two world wars.

No one listened. The British connection in Canada had lost its sea, land, and air arms. Now the armed forces were truly Canadian not British, and could best be used right here at home — against those at home — as Canadian nationalists had always insisted they should be, and as Trudeau did, in the October crisis.

Pierre Elliott Trudeau knew that unless one bashes Brits at home and abroad, one simply ends up bashing one's own country or oneself. This was a lesson best taught by those more Trudeau than Elliott. But it was a tough lesson for Trudeau to teach to others. In English Canada Trudeau the Brit-basher survived only because he offered unity and competence, even without a gut understanding of English Canadians, while the Tories only offered the shrinkability of Stanfield and the klutziness of Clark.

Still, in English Canada Trudeau lost to these two walking vapours in 1972 and 1979. In the land of the Anglos, Trudeauphobia — sheer hatred of P.E.T. and all his policies — soon became the normal way to view Trudeau. But in the sense of leaving a political legacy in Anglo Canada, a legacy Liberalism can ride to future victories, P.E.T. is *all* Trudeau and zero Elliott.

This supposedly "more Elliott than Trudeau," this fifteenth prime minister, knows less about English Canada than any other prime minister in Canadian history.

Trudeau's political French forebears present no such problem. Laurier was a full-fledged Gladstonian Liberal, better steeped in Adam Smith, Ricardo and Cobden than practically anyone in the Empire. Laurier's English oratory was far more skilled, his use of English and his English pronunciation far better than that of Pierre Elliott Trudeau.

Trudeau's audience was always primarily French; his message to the Québécois was always federalism: French power in the cabinet and in the civil service, Trudeau maintained, is real power; separatism is the powerlessness and isolation of the tribe. Trudeau never ever pleaded with the English; he didn't have to, for he knew that with the Québécois under control, Anglo capital investment and jobs would inevitably flow.

Laurier's audience was always the English. It was Laurier who bordered on Uncle Tomism, a Quebec heresy the supposedly more-Elliott-than-Trudeau has never embraced. Laurier, the protector of his people, was always peddling their bucolic virtues to the English tycoons of his day. Instead of the blessings of tycoonery Trudeau has given the Québécois the state itself to play with. Trudeau's appeals to the English on behalf of the French have been zero. A single Trudeau cabinet contains two to three times as many francophones as any King cabinet and, more to the point, any St. Laurent or Laurier cabinet. Trudeau has given the Québécois French power; they now need no Uncle Toms.

St. Laurent, like Laurier, was more Elliott than Trudeau. St. Laurent's full acceptance of conscription ended the crisis of 1944, but as an act it's more Elliott than Trudeau.

Despite what the Rosedale Radicals may say, Trudeau was the best informed, the most concerned and most involved federal francophone leader the Québécois have had. Conversely, there was Trudeau's pervasive ignorance of Anglo-Saxon Canada. The English component of Trudeau's cabinets were the weakest in history. Trudeau was the first prime minister so ignorant of Anglo-Saxon Canada he had to have advisers to tell him what English Canada really wanted. Laurier, the trained apostle of Gladstonian Liberalism, needed no interpreter of the English Canadian mind whispering in his ear.

St. Laurent, corporate counsel to English Big Business, was Howe's equal partner in English Canada, not his pupil. But for the man described as being more Elliott than Trudeau, someone had to explain the Elliott to the Trudeau. Explaining the Anglo-Saxon West and cosmopolitan Toronto to Trudeau was the No-no Nanton Kid, Jim Coutts, and Tom Axworthy.

Trudeau's overwhelming Frenchness and total lack of Elliotticity stands out in sharp relief when the image of Lester B. Pearson is projected on the rear screen of history. Of Pearson it would have been even sillier to say he was more Bowles than Pearson. But Pearson was as ignorant of French Canada as Diefenbaker and the whole population of Moose Jaw put together. Yet Pearson never resorted to a French Coutts to survive and Pearson's victories in Quebec were certainly within Trudeau's range. To Pearson Quebec was one more foreign country that a good diplomat handled through dispatches and cables, not Couttses and gurus.

It was also a total lack of Elliotticity that made it impossible for Trudeau to understand why Western Canada was pro-American. Was it simply because the West knew that Toronto and the East was pro-British? Or did geographical proximity make the West love Fargo, Sioux Falls and Butte more than Manchester or Birmingham? In part that hypothesis was true, but Trudeau's ignorance of English Canada meant an outlook that was equally Samsonian in its blindness to Western Canada and the teeming huddled Anglo-Saxon masses of the Golden Horseshoe. It was because he was much more Trudeau than Elliott that he could and did find Western Ontario as big a mystery as Western Canada.

Both places had one thing in common, a thing that made Trudeau uncomfortable; both were Anglo-Saxon in ethnic makeup

Seeking shelter under the umbrella of the British monarch was not quite the way Trudeau turned on the British connection.

Trudeau bashed Brits with a fervour during the constitution battle, though by 1982 Britannia was far more a spent force than a moral one.

Trudeau walks under the Old Flag as the Old Man, whose lifelong politics finally broke the back of Anglo-British supremacy in this country.

At the 1969 St. Andrew's Ball in Montreal, the kilted P.E.T. is at last more Elliott than Trudeau.

As usual there is no shortage of Celtic-Saxon beauties to admire the prime minister's sartorial toast to British-Canadian fun and games.

Top-hat Trudeau jauntily inspects the honour guard of the Honourable Artillery Company at Guildhall.

For Trudeau the pomp and circumstance of the British heritage was desirable; its historical substance and effective significance were not.

Trudeau's most secret love affair was with Canada's champion Britophile, John George Diefenbaker.

Trudeau could hardly let his Québécois followers know that he so admired Diefenbaker — the man who had so bitterly fought bilingualism and all of Trudeau's works.
Trudeau loved Diefenbaker's passion, his wit, his patriotism. Both men stood for One Canada, both were single warriors, both loved to fight. Dief's mastery of Western Canada was, for Trudeau, at least a partial entrée into the moods and feelings of the Great Plains.

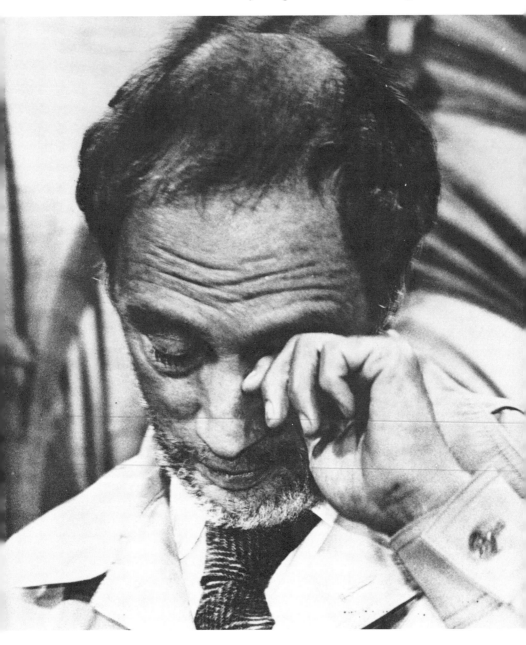

Dief's death cost the mourning Trudeau a friend, the one Westerner he truly respected and cared for.

and Anglo-Saxon in culture. The name Elliott was, after all, all there was Anglo-Saxon about Trudeau.

Of course, Trudeau, like all exotic outsiders, loved the symbolism of the West in the same way the King of Siam loved Anna's English customs and ways. Trudeau was always in seventh heaven when Otto Lang staged his annual Western barbecues in Ottawa. Trudeau loved being a Calgary Stampede marshal and went gaga at all the single-warrior combat he saw there.

Above all, Trudeau loved the West's number one single-combat warrior — John Diefenbaker. In particular, Elliott Trudeau saw in Campbell Bannerman Diefenbaker all the half-breed ambivalences he himself possessed. Diefenbaker had always argued that if his last name had been that of his mother, i.e., Campbell Bannerman, instead of that of his ethnic father, i.e., Diefenbaker, he would have been prime minister decades earlier. Dief's concern with his ethnic heritages was as deep as Trudeau's dualities. Under Diefenbaker the first Chinese became an MP, the first Indian a senator, the first Ukrainian a cabinet minister, and the first Jew a governor of the Bank of Canada. Dief the Cold Warrior was also the first prime minister to tear the Iron Curtain asunder so the voices of angry ethnic Canadians seeking freedom for their kith and kin could be heard in Kremlin halls.

Both men compensated for their ethnic defects as best they could. Diefenbaker did this by becoming the biggest Britophile in Canadian history. Sir John's Old Flag and Old Policy was merely a dress rehearsal for Dief's Last Stand for the British connection in Canada. Trudeau's Elliott stain was expunged by his being more a Québécois in every way than even the staunchest of separatists. The only concession to Elliott that Trudeau was prepared to make was the homage he paid to English beauty. Trudeau squired or showed off more Anglo-Saxon lovelies than Flo Ziegfeld, lovelies that certainly rivalled Jean and Olive, ethnic Diefenbaker's two British stock beauties.

If it be true that John Diefenbaker was more Campbell Bannerman than Diefenbaker, and P.E.T. more Trudeau than Elliott, it was equally true that both men stood for One Canada; indeed Dief regarded Trudeau's 1968 victory as vindication of his own 1967 One Canada stance. Had Diefenbaker lived he would certainly have bought the Trudeau Charter of Human Rights, for it was only Dief's Bill of Rights writ large.

Trudeau admired Dief the Parliamentarian; Dief admired Trudeau the Outrider's political skill in swallowing Pearson Liberals and NDPers before they swallowed him. Dief the Outsider lacked that Trudeau skill, having been aborted himself more than once by the Tory Establishment, and terminally bled by that same Establishment for most of his days.

While their differences were real — Dief was correctly convinced that Trudeau was out to scuttle the British connection — these two outsiders to the Canadian political process, one a paranoid, the other a relatively mirthless magus, actually liked one another. The biggest political mourner at Diefenbaker's epic funeral was Trudeau, who had lost an important ally for his constitution and his one entrée into Western Canada, Trudeau's one and only unrequited love.

They were an odd couple these two: One Solitude Diefenbaker who couldn't accommodate Quebec and Toronto and was done in by both, versus Trudeau the Third Solitude who couldn't accommodate the West politically but loved its culture and people almost viscerally. Dief lived on in the minds and hearts of his Prairie people. They and Trudeau both understood that Dief too was a single-combat warrior, a West Firster, who did his fighting to get something for others — his beloved plainsmen and the men in the sheepskin coats to whom Diefenbaker first gave security and then gave dignity.

Still a man more Elliott than Trudeau does not tell the West he won't sell their grain; or shout ''fuck you'' in the House of Commons at Tory MPs. Elliotts like Laurier and St. Laurent would never have had the nerve to declare War Measures or price and wage controls. Elliotts don't threaten to unilaterally patriate constitutions. Elliotts don't take on the whole world when they are in search of peace. In fact, Elliotts exist only in the chocolate-chip brains of Rosedale's radical Smarties.

For these chichi a PetroCan Trudeau will never be nationalist enough; a franco-Trudeau will not be French enough; a peacenik Trudeau will not be peaceful enough; a Diefenbaker-loving Trudeau will not be Western enough — but a War Measures Trudeau, there is now and there will always be plenty of.

On this latter point one finds oneself compelled to exit gracefully, leaving behind only this bone mot: Radical chichis of the world unite, you have nothing to lose but *vendu* Elliott Trudeau making you uptight.

4 The Movable Feast of Canadian Salon Socialism

What is remarkable about P.E. Trudeau is not that he was Canada's third French Canadian prime minister, or that he was the sixth Liberal to be first among equals; what is unique about Trudeau is that he was Canada's first socialist prime minister, without ever having been elected leader of the NDP, or having ever really compromised *his* socialist principles. This Trudeau conjuring was made possible by the supine co-operation of the Liberal Party of Canada led by Duck Supine himself, Lester Pearson. Pearson offered the Liberal party, its platform and its principles, for what they were, to a man they desperately wanted to run as a Quebec Liberal, yet who had only two years before condemned the Liberals as cowards, eunuchs, liars and cheats. The Liberal crime in Trudeau's eyes? They had broken their pledge to the country, and more important, pledges to Canadian socialists like Trudeau, Frank Scott, Michael Oliver and David Lewis, to keep nuclear arms out of Canada.

The Faustian Trudeau embraced the Satanic Grits; but certainly not their platform or their principles. In less than three years, Beat the Liberal Devils — at their own game — was Trudeau's favourite indoor sport. Trudeau kept his bargain with the Grits; he brought the Liberal Whore of Babble On the majority and spoils of victory — patronage, perquisites, prestige and naked unvarnished power. The Liberal serpent was thus content; it had got its share of rats to swallow even if it couldn't swallow one Pierre Elliott Trudeau.

This exercise taught Trudeau that socialism in Canada could only happen if socialists converted to Canada's only classless (i.e., lacking in class) society — the Liberal Party of Canada. The difference between the two parties — the NDP and the Trudeau Liberals — was never of principle or substance and really boiled down to a question of dollars and sense. The NDP got their dollars and most of their sense from the thousands of steelworkers and autoworkers who kicked in 15 cents a head per month for the party; while the Liberals, always a champion of minorities, did dunning ritual dances with a tiny band of corporate donors at $1,000s a head once a year.

In all key areas of stress, the Trudeau Liberals and Lewis-Broadbent forces coalesced and neither side cared if Trudeau were *really* a socialist or not. (Jean Marchand seemed to be the only one who did. To oral historian Peter Stursberg, Marchand swore up and down that Trudeau was "never ever" a socialist; presumably Marchand meant that Trudeau was never ever a *real* socialist like Bugs Bunny was never ever a *real* rabbit.) In 1972 the NDP propped up Trudeau's minority government; once again Trudeau was free to argue that in the Heavenly City of Liberalism the New Jerusalem was the best subdivision in the place. In 1974 the NDP parrotted Trudeau's attack on Stanfield's wage and price controls, and in the process nearly slid out of existence, as the angry voters rushed into Trudeau's back pocket to keep the Tories from emptying their front pockets. In 1980 the NDP committed internal hari-kari for Trudeau's constitution; once again the socialist backs were pinned firmly to the Trudeau Wall.

By 1984 the Trudeau Wall had become a wailing one. Trudeau, the most hated politician in Canada, was now paired off in a good portion of the public mind with the NDP, now the most hated third party in Canada since Diefenbaker squashed its predecessor, the CCF, in 1958. Trudeau had not exactly swallowed the NDP; the NDP had more or less fallen on swords of its own making.

By 1984 even Trudeau's enemies in the right wing of the Liberal Party were beginning to make eyes at Trudeau's old bedmates in the NDP. Envoys from Turner were promising Turner cabinet posts to Robert White of the United Automobile Workers and to Roy Romanow, former Saskatchewan NDP attorney-general. By 1984 Trudeau the socialist had left the NDP virtually nothing it could call its own. Much as NDPers could and did brag, in the most fashionable Rosedale and Rockcliffe salons, that PetroCan and the Foreign Investment Review Agency were really socialist inspirations, the political audit was balanced only in favour of Trudeau. Trudeau's peace mission simply swamped the NDP's legitimate desires for peace (traditionally one of the NDP's biggest drawing cards); ironically enough, Trudeau seized the peace initiative so well no one in Canada of any consequence saw any real inconsistency in Trudeau's peace initiative being accompanied by Cruise missile testing. Only on Western Canadian issues did the NDP still have some independence from Trudeau, and only then by alienating their Eastern Canadian followers — an Eastern Canadian following that in large part was sympathetic to Trudeau's initiatives.

Rarely had a prime minister exercised such a close relationship with a third party: never before such a close relationship with a socialist party. King had some intimacy in social welfare matters with the CCF, but nothing substantive. Even King's seduction of the Progressives was done on a professional and pragmatic basis. Borden flirted with the Quebec nationalists, Diefenbaker and Pearson with the Créditistes. Trudeau's links with Canadian socialism, however, were of a unique kind. The roots of that relationship went back a long way.

Trudeau was not to the socialist manor born, just to the manor. His father — a rare thing, a millionaire Québécois entrepreneur — was also in the early 1930s that even rarer of things — an R.B. Bennett-Maurice Duplessis Conservative. Not for papa Trudeau the joys of from each according to his ability to each according to his needs. Papa Trudeau preferred the joys of from each what you can get, to each as little as you can give. Trudeau the Younger learned the value of a buck at his father's knee, and does not part easily with a buck now: apart from being a lousy tipper, Trudeau is a most reluctant taxpayer, no fan of high succession duties and no enemy of inherited wealth.

As a good socialist, however, Trudeau did enjoy spending the people's money on everything from participatory democracy to PetroCan, from bilingualism to bullet-proof Cadillacs. Trudeau's socialism came from neither home nor school; in contrast, David Lewis was to the picket line born and Menshevik-Jewish Bundist socialism reared; Tommy Douglas's socialism was Bible Belted, and the socialism of the Jaded Observer was Star of David crossed all the way. "Socialism," said the Jaded Observer's fanatic Labour Zionist daddy, "is too beautiful, too good a thing — for the Gentiles." The Jesuits who taught Trudeau agreed with the Jaded Observer that socialism was an international Jewish conspiracy. The particulars of socialism Trudeau's Jesuit teachers did not quite grasp. Their economic and social theories came from Acquinas and Loyola. The good fathers thought that Keynes were what Charlie Chaplin used in his act, that a Gross National Product was Camillien Houde, and that the Beveridge Report was an exposé of Pepsi's. The Jesuits at Jean de Brébeuf Classical College taught Pierre the value of elites (hardly a socialist concept) and mastery over one's person, self-control and discipline over one's body and soul at all times; exercising personal mastery, control and discipline over the bodies and souls of others both Trudeau and the Jesuits agreed was a desirable and natural extension in logic.

Trudeau's studies in the Sorbonne exposed him to no socialist heresies; his wanderings in the desert gave him only sand in his eyes and little in the way of raiding the Lost Ark of the Socialist Covenant. Brief exposure to Britain's Marxist Mahatma Harold Laski did make something of a Red Tory of the Young Trudeau, much as a similar small exposure turned Dalton Camp from a Mackenzie King Liberal into a Red Tory too, and turned J.F.K. from an isolationist-reactionary into a New Dealer.

Trudeau's socialist mentors were all Canadians. His socialism was really quite weak — because the socialists he admired were weak socialists. Eugene Forsey was one such weak socialist.

Socialist Forsey's all-time hero was Arthur Meighen, whose chief stock in trade was imprisoning socialists, including the father of Canadian socialism, J.S. Woodsworth. In radical circles in the 1930s, '40s and '50s, socialists wondered what was more dangerous — Forsey's conservatism masquerading as socialism or Meighen's Red-baiting of socialists masquerading as small-c conservatism. Trudeau's other socialist mentor was Professor Michael Oliver, ex-president of the NDP and Carleton University. Westmount-born and parsonage-reared, Michael Oliver's socialism was so watered down the International Joint Commission declared it a Great Lake.

Trudeau's strongest socialist influence came from the goodness and dignity of Thérèse Casgrain, Quebec's most famous feminist and the daughter of one of Quebec's most distinguished Tories, and poet and legal scholar Frank Scott. Many a socialist tip was also picked up by Trudeau from Jean-Louis Gagnon, later an Information Canada czar, whose watertight socialism made him one of the most radical Québécois of his generation. Yet here too the socialist influence on Trudeau was marginal, leaving Trudeau at best the marginal socialist man. If, in St. Laurent's phrase, socialists were Liberals in a hurry, Madame Casgrain and Frank Scott were socialists so moderate they seemed to be in no hurry at all; in short, they'd rather walk than ride to the New Jerusalem.

Trudeau's socialism was not only weak but often there was more baloney than ham to it. Trudeau's bearded Christ-like appearance on the Asbestos picket line in 1949, and his inflammatory speeches there, were often more the stuff of nationalist rhetoric than the substance of socialism. At a time when the evils of ethnic nationalism had caused World War II, and socialists the world over were fighting ''national socialism,'' Trudeau was the perfect Québécois nationalist when he opposed conscription and supported Jean Drapeau, then the epitome of Quebec nationalism, for a seat in the House of Commons.

Indeed at that time, 1942, barely twenty-two years of age, Trudeau's nationalism was identical to that of the Godfather of today's separatism, René Lévesque. Both Trudeau and Lévesque were far from cowards; yet both men refused to enlist. Both saw World War II as still another exercise in British colonialism and imperialism, one in which the French Canadians would do a hell of a lot of the fighting, factory producing and dying, while the British and the British Canadians would get all the profits and all the glory. Both men were determined that the British sun *would* set on Quebec shores.

Lévesque's "hard" socialism at least told him that Hitler was a worldwide menace, that de Gaulle was better than Pétain, and that the Americans had never exploited the French in North America as had the British. Blending nationalism, socialism and Brit-bashing, Lévesque went off to do propaganda work, sometimes under rough wartime conditions, for the Americans.

Trudeau's "soft" socialism and internationalism was so weak in comparison to Lévesque's radicalism that, like the Irish and Hindu nationalists, he never heard the sound of Nazi goosesteps, only the sound of the British lion's roar. Trudeau was convinced French Canadians would have to help silence this roar if they were ever to be a truly free and proud people. Though at the time many of Trudeau's closest neighbours and friends were Jewish, and he became easily the biggest Judaeophile prime minister in our history, Trudeau understood very little about the perculiar horrors inherent in Nazism; consequently neither the scourge of the swastika nor Trudeau's own Jewish sympathies moved him to fight in World War II.

In this Trudeau was typical of most Quebec intellectual youth of the period. They were nationalist and insular, unaware of Nazism, trained at school to be sympathetic to Mussolini and to be in raptures over Pétain, and certainly ill-prepared for any understanding, never mind a proper one, of the seminal events of this century. Trudeau was no coward, no traitor, just a naive nationalist Quebecker in intellectual transit to the permanent truths that Laski, Frank Scott and Acton would soon give him. Still, in wartime, as in Asbestos years ahead, Trudeau's passion and basic Frenchness had once again overcome his supposed devotion to the reason of federalism, internationalism and anti-ethnic nationalism, the special socialist ideals Trudeau would adopt in the early 1950s. In the 1940s the call of blood for Trudeau was very strong. In the '70s and '80s, despite One Canada, despite being branded more Elliott than Trudeau, this supposed Uncle Tom and *roi nègre*, was far more nationalist in approach and ideology than Laurier and St. Laurent combined, and much closer to Lévesque than either man would care to admit.

In 1917 Laurier reluctantly fought conscription so he could play the shepherd to his fanatical French flock. In 1944 St. Laurent delivered a Québécois sheep to conscriptionist Canada with all the finesse of a Judas goat. Trudeau, who stayed at home, opposed conscription more vociferously and forcefully than even Lévesque, who was busy with his propaganda work in the United States. In the 1940s Trudeau the nationalist was even more truly *Québec aux Québécois* than Lévesque. In the '70s and '80s Trudeau the federalist One Canada socialist was still in so many, many ways more truly Québécois than the future separatist premier of Quebec. Certainly, at no time was Trudeau playing Quebec's Trotsky to Lévesque's Stalin.

To Trudeau there was no contradiction between his passionate commitment to all things Québécois and his commitment to Canada, between his pride of race and his socialist desire for a planned world social order. The keys to unravelling these apparently contradictory mysteries lay with Trudeau and his all-consuming passion for the concept and philosophy of nationalism. Trudeau, who had quite irresponsibly beaten the tom-toms of Quebec ethnicity on behalf of the asbestos strikers and Drapeau, was by 1968 the most convinced and efficient exorciser of Quebec nationalistic dybbuks in the land. Trudeau's belated hatreds of ethnic-based nationalisms, Quebec's as well as France's, Germany's or England's, was by the 1950s natural to one whose Frenchness was diluted by the call of Elliott blood. Québécois hatred of Anglo-Saxons and Jews was anathema to the half-breed Trudeau. Trudeau's childhood responses to playground teasing about his incomplete Frenchness raised in him the beginning prejudices against nationalism; they were soon fortified and rationalized for him by the writings of Hans Kohn and Elie Kadourie.

To Kohn and Kadourie nationalism was the bacillus from which holocausts are hatched; that these views came from two prominent Jewish academics made Trudeau, a lifelong Judaeophile, all the more convinced that what they had to say was right. In Trudeau's view the Chosen People had always been chosen as the victims of nationalism's worst excesses; to Trudeau the Jews were the best lie detectors of the virus of xenophobia and their scholarship in that area was the best organized and most insightful. Once Trudeau agreed with Kohn-Kadourie that ethnic nationalism was indeed the bacillus, then Lord Acton's espousal of the multi-racial state and the felicities of federalism was quickly embraced. Forms of socialism that were also heavily laced with call-of-blood, like Labour Zionism and the socialism of the Quebec separatists, Trudeau refused to buy. The socialism Trudeau embraced was the socialism of internationalism, of the United Nations, of foreign aid, North-South, the socialism of the brotherhood of man, a socialism that was more an apostolic mission than grubby economics and statism.

In his days as editor of the anti-Duplessis journal *Cité libre*, Trudeau was already a socialist, but it was a socialism of Trudeau's distinctly smudged stamp. His fight against Duplessis did concern itself with Duplessis's Red-baiting, union-busting and the generally poor working conditions in Quebec; still, the base of Trudeau's intellectual operations was the conventional critiques of democratic socialism. Trudeau's book on the asbestos strike, *La Grève de l'amiante*, has more statistics, economic jargon and pancake panaceas of social democracy than could be found in Keynes, Marx and the Forsey-Scott-Underhill League for Social Reconstruction put together. Trudeau, while still a good soft socialist and seeking some sort of living, did also practise labour law on behalf of Jean Marchand's Confederation of National Trade Unions; in the process Trudeau frequently encountered, and lost certification cases to, one David Lewis, a very "hard" socialist, representing the CNTU's antithesis, the Quebec Federation of Labour.

But all the time Trudeau was convinced that socialism, especially the Anglo-Saxon non-Marxist variety, could translate easily into the Quebec picture and thus help Quebec's working classes. The latter were sick — and the infectors were the Church, Duplessis and nationalism. In essence *Cité libre* was challenging Quebeckers to drop their racism, their economic passivity and their church-ridden taboos. *Cité libre* was asking the Québécois to look up to and live by the light of Forsey, Scott, Casgrain, Kohn, Kadourie and Laski — and of course the lightbulbs would be provided by Trudeau and *Cité libre*.

The social and moral aspects of socialism Trudeau had bought long ago. Unlike his Jesuit teachers, Trudeau knew that the welfare statism of the Beveridge Report in postwar Britain would not only challenge but save his Québécois generation. Trudeau knew too that the moral purpose issues the socialists were pushing were right: that women were entitled to legalized abortion and speeded up divorce; that nuclear arms in Canada were an obscenity; that socialists like Scott, Lewis and Forsey had provided what small semblance of civil liberties Canadians could call their own. Trudeau also knew that it was these same socialists who, more than members of any other political party, shared then and would in the future his fight for entrenching these same civil liberties in a Bill of Rights.

But while Trudeau was a social-issues-and-moralist socialist and wrote about that kind of socialism incessantly in *Cité libre* in the 1950s, he wasn't then or ever, despite the National Energy Program and PetroCan, an economic nationalist-socialist. In him socialism was basically moral and spiritual, a secular priesthood of the pure-at-heart, not the drab Marxist bookkeeper approach of nationalized American branch plants and controlled American cash flows. Trudeau has never been a Marxist and never viewed society as either class-divided or as class-conflicted. In Trudeau's One Canada, class harmony was in and the class struggle was out.

As the prime minister who trotted out wage and price controls that were really only wage controls, Trudeau was in no way acting in contradiction to *his* own deeply held socialist beliefs. In

Trudeau's view, controls were an indispensable tool for the good socialist state in the War Against Inflation, Part Two; as Trudeau saw it, inflation cannibalized all Canadian classes relatively equally, even threatening his own class and the very substance of his millionaire inheritance. In this particular scenario Trudeau's socialism was at its weakest. Even free enterprisers like C.D. Howe and Bob Winters couldn't have beaten Trudeau the pseudo-socialist at this most unsocialist game.

Traditional socialist economics were certainly not Trudeau economics, be those Trudeau economics price and wage controls or economic nationalism. Trudeau did not share the economic Canada Firstisms of left-wing Walter Gordon Liberals and Lewis socialists. Indeed Trudeau had no hesitation, as did Pearson, in standing up to Gordon, the Committee for an Independent Canada and the *Toronto Star* in this vital policy area. Trudeau seemed in 1968 to welcome a free and rapid flow of American investment into Canada.

Being a Québécois anti-nationalist, Trudeau saw Gordon and Mel Watkins as simply leading Canadian Anglos against American Anglos. Traditionally, Quebec preferred the gringos as bosses to the Anglo-Canadian stiff upper lipniks of Bay and St. James Streets. Ending American control of the economy, Trudeau knew, would not end Quebec separatism, the country's number one malaise; indeed it might have a countervailing effect and help separatism grow. Anglo-Canadian control of the economy would only convince the Québécois that the dour *maudits anglais* were even more in control of their lives than the gung ho, rather jovial Americans. Besides, Trudeau felt that really good Canadian businessmen didn't need government aid, and should handle the Americans on a single-combat-warrior basis.

Trudeau had only to point to his father as the best proof of the validity of this thesis. Trudeau's father had loved doing business with America; Trudeau's inheritance was due to the sale of his father's chain of gas stations to the Rockefellers. The Trudeaus received a good deal, and not surprisingly Trudeau the Younger did not feel the Damn Yankees were leading Canada down the road to perdition. Nationalization of "the commanding heights of the economy," a theme pushed by both the Regina Manifesto and the Waffle, was certainly not music to Trudeau's ears.

Bizarrely, his stand on Waffle Socialism and economic nationalism was the one time that Trudeau earned the grudging respect of big business, and their fastest guns in the West, not to mention the support of Quebec's business and social elites. Since this was really Trudeau's only major deviation from the basic tenets of Canadian socialism, his heresy was soon forgotten if not forgiven. Given Trudeau's surprise conversion to economic nationalism with PetroCan and the National Energy Program, his old heresies received complete absolution from Canadian socialists, who were once again lining up for free bed and board from the Born Again Socialist, Pierre Elliott Trudeau.

In both the areas of nationalization of industries and economic nationalism, Trudeau was certainly closer to Mitchell Sharp than he was to Lewis or Gordon. While many Babbitt businessmen hated Trudeau, particularly after he pronounced the free marketplace dead, Trudeau himself always liked businessmen, especially wild and woolly Western ones, because his father had been as wild and woolly an entrepreneur as they were. Smart businessmen knew that: Paul Desmarais and Power Corporation loved him; Ian Sinclair and the Canadian Pacific smiled benignly on him (and Sinclair was duly rewarded with a senatorship); and Canadian Jewish wealth, the Kofflers, Creeds, Bronfmans and Reichmans, adored this magus as if he were the Christ child itself.

Trudeau never feared capitalism or American investment. He was pro-union but never really ever against free enterprise. Trudeau's conversion to economic nationalism was surprising, and as strange a conversion as Bob Dylan's on the road from Nashville. *Cité libre* under Trudeau rarely talked of Marx, foreign investment or nationalization. What it did talk of, apart from social issues like abortion or nuclear arms for Canada, was the ethnic social disease of separatism and the cures for it known as federalism and reason above passion.

In this stark battle in Quebec, Trudeau took his allies where he found them. The Communist Party was such an ally. It was the first Canadian political grouping to endorse completely Trudeau's line of One Canada; the Lewis-led NDP had come up with "special status," a concept that inevitably meant two Canadas. Two Canadas was the policy the Tories under Stanfield gave birth to, and alas were much too slow to abort. Only Trudeau, Diefenbaker and the Communists correctly chose One Canada.

Trudeau would never give his benediction to the heresies of special status and *Deux Nations*. Nor would P.E.T. forget that, apart from Frank Scott and the Trudeau radicals, the real fight against Duplessisism was led by the Reds, while Lewis's socialists were often preoccupied with fighting their hated communist enemies. Trudeau remembered that Lewis's inherited fanatical anti-communism made him run against the communist Fred Rose in the mid-'40s, in hopes of splitting the progressive vote and keeping a Red out of Parliament. To Trudeau, Lewis's attitude to the Reds was pure unalloyed socialist sectarianism: he saw Lewis as being almost as much a McCarthyite and Red-baiter as Duplessis.

Trudeau thought highly of the way the communists fought back against Duplessis's Padlock Laws, and the way they organized labour unions in clothing, aluminum and pulp and paper, despite the hostility of Duplessisism's state-supported vigilantes and goon squads, and despite the hostility of the Lewis socialists. Trudeau particularly admired the brilliance and courage of the Communist Party's underground activities in Nazi Europe.

Trudeau's attitude to the communists was not one of bourgeois romanticism; nor was Trudeau a fellow traveller or a dupe. Simply put, Trudeau saw nothing to fear in the Red Menace and saw nothing in Red Russia to make him shiver during the Cold War. Trudeau agreed with his fellow socialists and academics that though Soviet society was totalitarian, Russia was not "a clear and present" danger. As Trudeau saw it, only American over-reaction caused the Korean War, and only an American *idée fixe* on the domino theory brought about the Vietnam humiliation. In an uncanny resemblance to American isolationists of pre-World

War II and Munich appeasers like Mackenzie King, George Drew, Meighen and J.S. Woodsworth, Trudeau put the interests of Canada and Quebec above everything else and especially over what he felt was so-called Soviet aggression. Neither Korea, Hungary, Vietnam, Czechoslovakia, Afghanistan nor Poland, individually or collectively, had the moral force to bring Trudeau to a jihad against Moscow.

It is this attitude that led Trudeau to pooh-pooh the NATO alliance, the same alliance that David Lewis in full Cold War stride brutally force-fed to the CCF. Trudeau was certainly out of step with official Lewis socialism on his second visit to the Soviet Union. On that vainglorious occasion Trudeau praised a Gulag as good enough for him and suggested Ukrainian freedom fighters were simply terrorists like the FLQ back home. Trudeau couldn't see then and perhaps not even now the tastelessness of that thesis. Terrorism and ethnic nationalism went hand-in-glove in a good portion of Quebec, therefore Trudeau reasoned that ethnic nationalism in and of itself inevitably bred terrorism everywhere. Lewis, the son of a man driven out of Poland for his Jewish nationalist-Bundist views and later in life a Labour Zionist himself, could hardly put up with Russia's harrassment of Israel and the Jews. Lewis the Canadian socialist was never as naive about Russian communism as Trudeau. Lewis's handling of the Canadian communists may on many occasions have been rough but, always the better street fighter than Trudeau, Lewis knew that communism snuffs out democratic socialism first and freedom second. To Lewis, communism and socialism were no more compatible than Nazis and Jews, or Stalin and Trotsky. In this area of Cold War socialism, Trudeau and Lewis once again were Poles apart.

In one other area there was an ironic split between Trudeau's water-wings socialism and Lewis's New-But-In-Need-Of-Sand-blasting Jerusalem. Trudeau, the man whose behaviour gave birth to a thousand daily RCMP security suspicions, felt Red-hunting by the Security and Intelligence Division had to be placed on the back burner; the hunting and trapping of separatists was Trudeau's number one priority. Lewis, the cold warrior and fierce anti-communist, who nevertheless merited (according to CCF leader M.J. Coldwell and a 1966 Royal Commissioner on Security) the largest collection of active security risk files in the Horseman's security and intelligence branch, still differed sharply from Trudeau's socialism in this sensitive area of separatist-bashing. Lewis was not as alarmed as Trudeau about the ethnic nationalism of Quebec separatists, for Lewis was an ethnic nationalist himself. True, Lewis deplored the anti-Semitism and hatred of Anglos implicit in much of Québécois nationalism, and was certainly in secret sympathy with Trudeau's rigorous bloodletting of that oldest and worst of political diseases. Moreover, Trudeau's stand on the sensitive matter of separatist racism had by 1968 made Lewis, the original special statusnik, an ardent supporter of Trudeau's One Canada.

Still, Lewis the Red-baiter would not go along with separatist-bashing; Lewis the Red-baited still felt that the chief security menace to Canada was the Bolshevik one. In Lewis's eyes, the Red Star Over Canada, not separatism, still deserved the Horseman's top priority. This Trudeau-Lewis clash on socialist dogma was clearly the most ironic battle between the two titans ever; it was certainly the most bizarre.

The relationship between Trudeau socialism and Canadian (which is mostly Lewis) socialism may have been Odd Couplish and Siamese Twinned but it does raise the best of all the Great Questions. If David Lewis on numerous occasions asked son Stephen, Is Trudeau good or bad for the Jews?, surely they must have asked themselves this Great Question too: Is Trudeau good or bad for Canadian socialism?

The answers to that apparent riddle are actually straightforward enough. Trudeau was enormously helpful to Canadian socialism in acting as Lewis's beard, that is, in doing the dirty and rough jobs the NDP lacked the power and (if they had the power) the balls to do. Ottawa insiders contended that no one was a more fervent *secret* admirer of War Measures than David Lewis. In the October Crisis Trudeau saw the FLQ as incipient Fascism;

Lewis, aware of the FLQ's vicious anti-Semitism and racism, upped the ante a bit. According to Lewis the FLQ was Nazism on the march.

Lewis hoped to inherit Trudeau's 1968 "bleeding heart" vote gone forever from Trudeau with the wind of War Measures; by 1970 the "bleeding hearts" were all in bleeding NDP country to stay. Where the "bleeding hearts" went the radical chichi were sure to follow; by 1970 post-War Measures English Canada's Brightest and Best were all in permanent rest and recreation in Lewis's armed socialist camp. Still, Lewis was the one socialist chieftain who had secretly relished every Trudeau attack on the "bleeding hearts" not only because he now had their votes in the bag but because he shared Trudeau's contempt for the arrogance, hypocrisy and moral relativism of the radical chichi — the most dangerous subspecies of Canadian socialism.

War Measures was only one case where Trudeau had bailed out Lewis socialism. His One Canada policy was another. The NDP, if it stood for anything at all, stood on guard for a strong central government to fight big business and Uncle Sam. For the socialist centralizers to give special status to Quebec (as they did) was even for these ruthless pragmatists on the Left a contradiction in terms; soon the media and academics would force them to conclude that special status had made the NDP the laughing stock of Canadian politics. Trudeau's same-as-always status for Quebec was another godsend for the NDP. If the francophone Trudeau Liberals and senior partners in the democratic Left could go for Canadian Wholeness then surely the Anglo-Saxon junior partners of the Canadian democratic Left, the NDP, could plausibly and swiftly dump special status and embrace the respectability of Trudeau's stubborn federalism.

English Canadian liberals, and even some Liberals, might condemn Trudeau's One Canada as a mere smoke screen for putting Quebec in its place, but the NDP was grateful for it. Once again the NDP could strongly support a Trudeau position, one that brought them internal peace as they quietly watched the sunset on special status shores. The aimless NDP was now happy,

"If you get us the NDP, I'll get you the Liberal Party."

This perhaps is what power broker Mitchell Sharp is whispering to Trudeau at the 1968 Liberal leadership convention. Sharp, by withdrawing from the race and throwing the weight of the Old Liberal Establishment behind radical Trudeau, made him prime minister.

Powerhouse Maryon turns on beaming Pierre as the Pearsons congratulate Canada's first socialist prime minister. Lester Pearson's benevolent silence conferred political consent.

The mouse rides the elephant for the first time. It is a rough ride. For Trudeau, radical Liberals and socialists, no issue burns hotter than Canadian-American relations.

Still, Trudeau won't hear of any radical rhetoric about bad old Uncle Sam.

Although P.E.T. did find Bonzo easier to embrace than President Reagan.

Dealing with Bonzo was also easier than keeping Canadian nationalists happy and onside.

But to disarm the NDP, Trudeau simply stole one of their giants...

. . . and their major issue: disarmament. The global conciliator speaks at the United Nations.

for Trudeau had given them a Quebec policy they could live with in their B.C., Prairie and Ontario francophobe and bigot strongholds. Indeed, indirectly Trudeau had given the NDP the only toe-hold it would ever have in Quebec. In Quebec, where the NDP had never elected a soul and had lost more deposits than the banks in the Great Depression, Trudeau Liberals like Pelletier, Marchand, DeBané and Joyal gave the democratic Left the only relevance it had ever had in that "peculiar" province.

The NDP was as bereft of imagination in the constitutional area as it was on One or Two Canadas. Having no policy of its own that could satisfy both the NDP bosses of the East and populist-socialists of the West, the NDP establishment bought Trudeau's constitution policy at a special discount. In this game where Trudeau was easily the master, he won in the NDP a powerful ally at a crucial time; the NDP in turn nearly choked to death on its Western gripes of wrath. In fairness to the NDP, necessity drove them to the Trudeau constitution. The centripedes of the NDP knew that going Trudeau might lose them one third of their legs in the West; not going Trudeau would mean amputation of fifty per cent of their legs in Ontario, where the party was already facing oblivion. Still, whatever the NDP motives were on the constitution, Trudeau was neither good nor bad for Canadian socialism; he was simply its master.

On the whole though, Trudeau was a definite plus for Canadian socialism, NDP style: both when he was on his socialist best behaviour and when he was most certainly not. When Trudeau in minority brought in PetroCan, the NDP quite unfairly took full credit, as the CCF had for Mackenzie King's old age pension scheme. When Trudeau blurted out his socialist truisms that the free marketplace had suddenly passed away and free enterprise was on death row, the result was a national wing-ding debate on socialism in which Trudeau fought without any help from the socialists, and came out the clear loser.

Big business and its kept pigeons, the Tory Party, and Les Media Mini-Minds were so busy focusing debate on whether Trudeau was *really* a socialist and were so shrill in attacking the evils of Trudeau the socialist, they completely overlooked Canada's official socialist party, the NDP. No media biggies wanted to ask Ed Broadbent if he were *really* a socialist; they didn't want to ask the NDP anything. Untouched by this furore of the late '70s, Broadbent came out of bed with Trudeau as Mr. Clean on that one. The NDP was declared by the media to be the one true socialist party, the only true alternative to monopoly finance politics in Canada. Trudeau socialism was dismissed as either opportunism or perversion. Thus at a very crucial time Trudeau returned to the NDP a semblance of relevance which hitherto had all but disappeared.

When Trudeau was at his worst social behaviour, once again the NDP came up in clover. In 1972, as Trudeau listened intently to the Mantovani sound of his critical path flows, lectured his bureaucrats on "crisis management" and said "amen" to genetic engineering, regional desks and the War on Inflation, he decided that what he was running on Parliament Hill was a successful business enterprise, led by himself and the country's best political-social-economic management team. In the election of 1972 Trudeau and his business administration school advisors ran a campaign worthy of R.B. Bennett and John Bracken. Trudeau moved so far right he fell right out of the democratic Left and into the vortex of Power Corporation capitalism. At last the NDP, for the first time since the dawning of the Age of Trudeau, had most of Canadian socialism all to itself. With "corporate welfare bums" as the rallying cry, the NDP was finally the senior partner in the democratic Left; it won a record total of thirty-one seats and Lewis had waged the democratic Left's best and most modern campaign ever. Knowing that Trudeau had to move Left to live, the NDP also knew that they alone had the only working wheelchair in left-of-centre Canada. That wheelchair was their promise of support for Trudeau in the House. That deal was one neither the NDP nor Trudeau could really refuse to accept.

Finally, Trudeau was good for Canadian socialism because only he could and did offer the socialists the perquisites of rewards and appointments that they, as perpetual losers, would otherwise never get. In the funniest of all ironies surrounding the Trudeau-NDP relationship, Trudeau was the NDP's number one bagman and patronage dispenser. The list of Trudeau's gifts to the junior partner of Canadian socialism is both long and impressive. Sent by Trudeau to the Canadian Senate were the illustrious socialists Forsey and Casgrain. Sent to Information Canada was watertight socialist Jean-Louis Gagnon. Former B.C. NDP leader Tom Berger was called to the bench; so too was John Gilbert, NDP MP, and John Osler, ex-CCF candidate and former law partner of David Lewis. Under Trudeau, Ted Jolliffe, Lewis's other partner, and a man who led the Ontario CCF to within three seats short of power at Queen's Park in 1943, was made chairman of the public service Staff Relations Board. The legendary Ostrys, the Eleanor and Franklin of Canadian socialism, were both made deputy ministers. Former premier Tommy Douglas's socialist advisors, Tom Shoyama and Al Johnson, were made deputy ministers and Big Al received the ultimate accolade of the CBC presidency.

The New Left wing of Canadian socialism got its reward too. Even when named as members of the Extra Parliamentary Opposition by the excitable Jean-Pierre Goyer, New Lefties in Ottawa found their way into the highest bureaucratic offices in the land and on some of its most prestigious inquiries and commissions.

But the most impressive symbol of the fluidity of Trudeau and NDP socialism and their symbolic relationship was an appointment that thoroughly legitimized the democratic Left in the eyes of Canada. The placing of the lion and the unicorn in the hands of Manitoba's first socialist premier was Trudeau's *coup de grâce*. Ed Schreyer became the first and probably the last socialist governor-general in Canadian history. He was also the first ethnic and the first Western governor-general in Canadian history. In one stroke Trudeau rewarded Canadian socialism for its unswerving loyalty to him, proved his own patchwork quilt of multiculturalism did cover all the political bases and told at least the ethnic West that he really did give a damn about their feelings.

None of these remarkable acts, all good for Canadian socialism, could ever have been carried off by the impotent NDP. Those Trudeau appointments opened Rideau Hall, the Senate, the Bench and the Mandarinate to the best and brightest in Canadian socialism. Without Trudeau all this first-class socialist talent would have remained only a beam in David Lewis's blind eye, and in L.B.J.'s phrase, would have been outsiders pissing into the Trudeau tent, rather than inside pissing out.

But if one pushed the down-side button in Trudeau's relations with the NDP, then the Trudeau bedding of the socialists, with their clipped ejaculations and constrained climaxes, simply proved that in the democratic Left it was all power and passion to the Trudeau Soviet and a so-so joy ride for the standard brand of Canadian socialism. The Jaded Observer had on a previous occasion put it quite succinctly: "For the NDP to be in bed with the Liberals is like getting oral sex from a shark."

When Trudeau was bad, the Tories, not the NDP, corralled the good. The NDP claimed PetroCan, but Trudeau legislated it into existence and the history books agreed. Trudeau's National Energy Program left the NDP bereft of an energy policy of their own. Trudeau's Trojan Horse constitution turned the NDP into Trudeau "me-tooers" in the East and Lougheed "me-tooers" in the West. The revolt by Alan Blakeney and Lorne Nystrom so split the NDP that the Trudeau shark now saw the possibility of swallowing the Ontario NDP minnows leaving the Western NDP drifting aimlessly in dustbowl orbit over miles of unpaved Saskatchewan road. Trudeau's 1984 peace initiative, one which even John Turner over and over again promised not to touch, leaves the Liberal Party, not the NDP, in the vanguard of this most attractive vote-getting issue.

Trudeau, who neither in 1968 nor in 1972 ever dreamt the impossible dream of a tame Canadian socialism playing His Master's Voice to a reform Trudeau Liberal Party, was by 1984 dreaming that dream in technicolour. By 1984 Canadian socialism had often flitted in and out of bed with the Trudeau Liberals; by 1984 Canadian socialism was half smothered to death by the soft downy pillows of 24 Sussex Drive.

Trudeau has been *doing* it to the NDP from the very beginning. In 1968 he took away from Lewis the two people who had given socialism its only credibility in Quebec — Thérèse Casgrain and Frank Scott. The creative intellectuals of Toronto who had once supported the NDP, and historians like Ramsay Cook, J.T. Saywell, J.L. Granatstein, who would have gone NDP had Winters won in 1968, bought the divinity of Trudeau and the Liberals as their predecessors Underhill and King Gordon had found their false god in Pearson.

Even when Trudeau was having two-way sex with the NDP, an extended foreplay that propped up Trudeau's minority government for two years, it was Lewis, not Trudeau, who was accused of sexual deviation. The same charge was levelled at Broadbent over the constitution. Trudeaumania almost killed the NDP as the socialist female faithful switched to Pierre. Trudeauphobia only made angry NDPers switch to the Tories. The ten-year NDP affair with Trudeau bled Canadian socialism as dry as a female hemophiliac in the arms of Dracula; there's very little socialist blood left to shed.

Still where there's spent sex the erection of new hope is possible. There was no lasting second sexual encounter between the Broadbent socialists and Trudeau, and there will not be another Liberal bedding of the NDP in the foreseeable future.

Broadbent socialism may indeed survive but near-fatal damage has already been done to it. In the movable feast of Canadian salon socialism, it is clear that Trudeau had eaten far, far more than he had been eaten. Trudeau's gluttony had stunted the growth of the NDP for decades to come. Given the rapid movement of Canadian socialism's movable feast, one is never certain whether Pierre Elliott Trudeau, canoeist, karateist or Zen Buddhist, had swallowed up the Liberal Party of Canada and the NDP holus-bolus or merely their heads and tails.

Socialism is a state of mind; Trudeau is now and has always been a state-of-mind socialist. State-of-mind socialists do not have to belong to socialist parties and certainly Trudeau was never a member of the NDP and probably never a member of the CCF; still Trudeau's socialism was only slightly to the right of David Lewis. Politicians lacking state-of-mind socialism can, nevertheless, be active, committed, engaged socialists. No man was freer of ideology than Roosevelt; no North American has ever been a more successful socialist. Ramsay MacDonald, the British state-of-mind socialist prime minister, was easily as conservative as Herbert Hoover. Ed Schreyer, the socialist premier of Manitoba who fooled around with state-run automobile insurance, a left-wing Liberal concept, was nothing more or less than a Jeffersonian liberal.

By 1984 there was nothing left of the Trudeau-Lewis-Broadbent alliance or understanding. But in 1984 Trudeau's own socialism was still alive and kicking. To Trudeau, socialism was the vindication and defence of Big Bureaucrat economic and social power. Trudeau's preoccupation with the future of high technology and the survival of Canada's aerospace industry was traditional socialism at work with a vengeance. Already the perfect Hamiltonian conservative in his perpetual bail-outs of Dome and big business, Trudeau's multimillion-dollar rescue of Canadair and de Havilland was simply proof positive that in Trudeau socialism, not only does the state guarantee the rules of the marketplace, the state guarantees the marketplace itself. In Trudeau socialism, the free market may be dead but only the state can be either its quickener or its undertaker.

In 1984 Trudeau was still the most successful socialist in Canadian history. The way the NDP was evanescing, Trudeau could very well be Canada's Last Best Socialist.

5 Meltdown in the Melting Pot

The legendary self-destructive Jewish-American satirist, Lenny Bruce, trying to distinguish between the melting-pot culture of New York City and the Yankee Anglo-Saxon culture of Sioux City, Iowa, said everyone in New York is by definition Jewish, be they Black, Welsh, Puerto Rican, the Road Runner, Italian, Irish or Jewish. Everyone in Sioux City, Iowa, said Mr. Bruce, was goyish (i.e., Gentile-square), be they Norwegian, Scottish, Transylvanian, German, Moravian or Jewish.

In the multicultural Canada of Pierre Elliott Trudeau, Lenny Bruce would have had a far easier time with his complex definitions: in Trudeau Canada, everyone from Green Gables to Jalna, from Cape Breton to Dawson City, everyone — including Wayne and Shuster, Layton and Cohen, Richler and Hirsch — is goyish.

The stark simplicity of the Bruce model works in Canada even better than it does in the United States. For our country, sad to say, is, culturally, as *judenrein* (free of Jews) as East and West Germany or Lapland. If one believes that a culture lacking in Jewish input lacks richness, soul and just plain depth, then English Canadian culture, whose only Jewish ingredients so far are the Montreal Smoked Meat Sandwich and Bronfmans' whiskey, is as barren as it is insular; it is a culture more fit for preserving whales, puffins and seals than for preserving the human spirit. This Canadian culture, bereft of Jewishness, and more proud of its forests, timber, fish and fur heritage than that of its racially diverse people, such a humourless culture, often turned in on itself, rarely hesitates to turn on others. Such an English Canadian culture can be, and quite often is, as xenophobic as a good deal of Québécois culture has been for centuries.

The Jews of Canada provide Canadians a prism through which to refract on at length. The shabby history of the Jews in Canada tells us a great deal about the shabby history of Canada itself. The resplendent treatment of Canadian Jewry by Pierre Elliott Trudeau equally tells us as much or more about our fifteenth prime minister than, say, his handling of War Measures or the Canadian continental shelf. Indeed Trudeau's love affair with the Jews is probably the maddest and most passionate fling that Trudeau has ever flung; of this love affair Lenny Bruce could only have observed that Canada may be goyish but Trudeau is certainly Jewish.

That Trudeau was their landsman, their Godfather at Ottawa court, their first *real* access to state power, the Jews of Canada would unblushingly have to agree. The list of talented Jews given their heads (and not on any platter either) in government, politics and the judiciary by Pierre Elliott Trudeau is endless. The late Chief Justice Bora Laskin was a historical first. So was Privy Councillor Herb Gray. So is Alan Gotlieb, the first of his faith to become undersecretary of state for external affairs. Jack Austin was the first Jewish principal secretary to a prime minister, and was later made a senator and the third Jewish Trudeau cabinet minister. (In painful contrast, Joe Clark's cabinet, caucus and office were virtually as *judenrein* as Outer Mongolia or Zimbabwe. Senators Jack Marshall of Newfoundland and Nathan Nurgitz of Winnipeg provided both Clark and Mulroney with their only Jewish content in caucus. Even at that, Marshall is a Trudeau appointee — one of five Jews he sent to the Senate.)

Jews held under Trudeau the top posts in the cabinet, in the bureaucracy and the judiciary. Apart from Laskin, Trudeau appointed a Jewish Chief Justice in B.C., Manitoba, Quebec and Nova Scotia, and a Jewish Associate Chief Justice in Alberta. Also named were additional Jewish federal justices in B.C., Alberta and Saskatchewan, Nova Scotia (two), Manitoba (six),

Quebec (10) and Ontario (19). And Maxwell Cohen was sent to the International Court of Justice in the Hague. Under Trudeau far more than the proverbial Jewish minyan-ten held deputy ministerial or assistant deputy ministerial rank.

The social climate created by Trudeau was more than mere tolerance; it was an actual joyous acceptance of Jewish talent. The precedent set by Trudeau's philo-Semitism now makes it unthinkable for the Conservatives, should they return to power, not to appoint Jews to the cabinet, the judiciary and the bureaucracy. Nor would John Turner dare to renounce Trudeau's attitude to the Jews. In fact few politicians are as close to the Jewish community as Turner. In the years of his exile, the *one* public event Turner eagerly embraced was a "concert and gala dinner of tribute in honour of Zubin Mehta" at the Sheraton Centre in Montreal, April 27, 1983. "The sponsoring organization was the Canadian Friends of the Hebrew University." The official sponsor "John N. Turner, PC, QC."

This climate of opinion generated by Trudeau made Bill Davis's Conservative government appoint the first and second Jews to the Ontario cabinet, the first Jew (Hugh Segal) to the office of Principal Secretary to the Premier, and the first Jewish deputy minister and minister team (Bernard Ostry, a former Trudeau deputy minister, and Larry Grossman) in Canadian political history.

(It is also no accident that Premier Davis is the most popular Conservative ever with Canadian Jewry. For Jews, Davis's Arab boycott and human rights legislation made Ontario not only a place to stand and a place to grow, but a place to dwell and a place to kvell. Davis's enthusiasm for Israel and affection for Canadian Jewry make him a close contender with Trudeau for the crown of Gentile King of the Jews. Nor is this pro-Israel stance a personal aberration on Davis's part; Davis's attorney general, Roy McMurtry, was quick to announce his all-out support for Israel's Lebanon adventure in the spring of 1982; McMurtry even went further than Davis — whose silence on the Lebanese caper was intriguing — by informing a Toronto Zionist rally in support of the Lebanese incursions that he, like St. Paul, was ''a Christian Zionist.'' McMurtry did not have to tell Toronto's assembled Jewry that his riding was half Jewish; they already knew.)

P.E.T.'s love of Jews made possible the election of seven Jewish MPs in the Trudeau era. The unstormy weather brewed up by the emancipator of Canadian Jews saw across Canada two NDP provincial leaders, one federal NDP leader, one NDP B.C. premier, two Ontario leaders of the opposition, one Manitoba Liberal leader, and one Manitoba Tory leader all accepted for high office despite, or perhaps because of, their Jewishness. With the gates of Trudeau's Rome opened in tribute to Jewish talent, the gates of the provinces could hardly be shut to the Ramadan delights of Jewish wit and wisdom.

This cultural and political explosion of Jewish talent in Canada would never have happened without Trudeau, Canada's first prime minister to have no fear of the Jews, and to hold no debilitating myths about them. Since his boyhood in Outremont, Trudeau had seen organized Jewry as a force for progress. Jews had been among Trudeau's closest allies in the fight against Duplessisism. His Montreal riding was almost 50 per cent Jewish, and always gave him whopping majorities. Trudeau's Jewish advisors, particularly H. Carl Goldenberg and Maxwell Cohen, were like blood brothers to him. Trudeau's turning on of Jewish Power followed inevitably from such close ties.

By comparison, in the 1930s Mackenzie King was so scared of the Jews moving into Canada and desecrating, among other things, the sacred relics and ruins of his Kingsmere summer home, that he made sure that none of the dying and doomed Jewish refugees would find sanctuary in Canada. King kept the Jews out. He could afford the luxury of his vicious anti-Semitism, for Drew and his fellow Tories were even worse anti-Semites than King was. King even kept the Jewish vote, crucified and castrated as it was by a Liberal party that knew how to play on Canadian Jewish fears, cowardices and Uncle Tom timidities, a vicious game that the Tories, in contrast, were most inept at.

Still, in all fairness, King's exclusion of the Jews from cabinet (a practice continued by St. Laurent) may have been due less to his overt or covert anti-Semitism than to his laws of politics. In King's ethnic balance-of-power cabinet making, talent always took second place to leverage; Canadian Jews, who were less than one per cent of the population, would never be allowed a cabinet seat that could be more profitably exploited through the appointment of an Ottawa Valley Irish Catholic or a bilingual bisexual Ukrainian Catholic from Winnipeg North.

Under Diefenbaker, the Chosen People were rarely chosen. Diefenbaker did make Louis Rasminsky the first Jewish governor of the Bank of Canada. But this hardly made the Chief a Jewish emancipator or even a social pioneer. In 1958, in the biggest landslide in Canadian history, Diefenbaker elected 208 Tories: one was Chinese, one was female and a fair number were Ukrainian; fifty were Québécois; but not one of the 265 Tories that ran, won or lost in 1958 was Jewish. Dief often proclaimed his sincere love of Israel, and in 1956 he defended Britain and Israel on the Suez question. By 1976, Diefenbaker had more orange groves named after him than Sunkist, but in Canada he had done little to exploit Jewish brain power. Unlike Trudeau, Diefenbaker was happier, indeed more comfortable, with Anglo-Saxons or, for that matter, Ukrainian Tory judges, senators and cabinet ministers than he was with Jews. The most charitable explanation for this preference was the Jews were too cultured, too urban, too liberal, hence too sophisticated for Dief's rustic populist tastes.

With Pearson, the diplomatic water-boy of the Western world, the velvet glove of diplomacy covered more often than not a double-dealing hand for Canadian Jewry. For the Jews of Israel, Pearson sent a condemnation of their Suez intervention, and armed UN peacekeepers. To the Jews of Canada, Pearson spoke in tongues pickled in empty rhetoric; Pearson's "Mid-East Peace In Our Time" sent Canadian Jewry empty promises in empty powder monkeys. In Pearson's minority elections of 1963 and 1965, only two Jews got elected. The famous Pearson survival kit Cell 13 (Walter Gordon, Keith Davey, Paul Hellyer, et al) that saved the Liberals from post-1957/58 extinction, boasted no Jewish names of any consequence. Pearson also kept his cabinet, bureaucracy and courts 99 and 44/100ths Ivory, Gentile, Pure: there were not many notable Jewish appointments during the Pearson years.

When it came to Jews, Pearson and Diefenbaker simply out-tokened one another; their tokenism only bred in desperate response more and more Jewish Uncle Tomism, be it of the sinuous Sigmund Samuel-Gentle Sam Bronfman variety or the even more joyous ball playing with the Canadian Establishment of Toronto Jewish mayors Nathan Phillips and Phil Givens. This was an edifying spectacle for neither Jew nor Gentile. Canadian Jewish talent responded to the sight of these sorry stigmata by emigrating to the U.S. in droves.

The Jesuit-Meritocrat Trudeau responded negatively to this display of Jewish lapdogism. Trudeau, in dealing with the Jews, preferred Thomism to Tomism. A proud man himself and one always seeking Acquinian natural justice, Trudeau was quick to spot in the Jews a proud people, unnaturally deprived of an outlet for their talents and skills. Trudeau was totally devoid of the personal and political insecurities of King, St. Laurent, Diefenbaker and Pearson. That quartet feared a backlash should Jewish talent be officially blessed by the state; Trudeau only wondered how the state could properly function without the fullest participation of Jews.

Equally remarkable was Trudeau's capacity to tilt Jewry's own racial laws in his own favour and get away with it. Not since King Ahasuerus took unto himself a Jewish wife, Queen Esther, has Jewry so applauded a Gentile head of state, indeed a philosopher king, toying so playfully with Jewish women. Both before his marriage and as late as his peace mission, Trudeau publicly displayed his affections for Barbra Streisand, seeming to delight in playing Yentl to her insouciant Yenta.

Less well known but far younger and more beautiful than Barbra Streisand is Trudeau's first Jewish Canadian Princess, Melissa Singer-Cohn. This Albertan was seen dancing an Israeli hora with

Trudeau (to a "standing ovation" by "cheering crowds") at the 1982 St. Valentine's Day Dance at the Beth Zion synagogue in Côte St. Luc in the very heart of Trudeau's Montreal riding. Ms Singer, a bit of a mystery woman, is best remembered for her flamboyant apparel that night — a lynx coat, black sequined jacket and evening pants. Ms Singer, it seems, shared with the prime minister a love of the law — in her case aerospace law, which she was studying at McGill University.

What is equally mysterious about this whole event is that it was never recorded in any regular major Canadian media outlet. It was seemingly a scoop by the *Canadian Jewish News*, whose joy at the story seemed to know no bounds — certainly not the bounds of traditional Jewish laws and customs on ethnic and racial matters.

But Trudeau's successful scuttling of Jewish totems and taboos on interracial dating were anything but a worrisome pattern. Trudeau's dalliances with Canadian Jewish Princesses were brief and well dallied. Trudeau was soon back to plucking the heart strings of talented Gentile beauties like guitarist Liona Boyd.

Still, Trudeau continued to remain as comfortable as an old shoe in the presence of the Jews; he let Jews write the press gallery dinner satire speeches he so dreaded to write and deliver; he let Jews find him the best new night spots in Toronto to visit; and he always took a goodly portion of Jewish advice on all matters urgent and necessary. Only two other North American heads of state, Franklin Delano Roosevelt and Harry Truman, had the rapport Trudeau has had with Jews.

In that observation lies a Tale of Two Jewish Cities so to speak — the Jewish City of God that lives on American Dreams and the Jewish City of the Bland Leading the Bland that is multi-cultural Canada. In the United States in the hundred years between the 1880s and 1980s, millions of Jews poured in; apart from some notorious setbacks, America made the Jews welcome. By 1980, American Jewry had single-handedly built ten world-class industries in their new home — the garment and fashion industry, the copper and uranium industries, mass circulation newspapers, the Macy and Gimbel department store chains, the Levi clothing empire, Broadway theatre, Hollywood film studios and network television — not to mention the intellectual industry of America per se. Hartt, Schaffner, Marx, Guggenheim, Pulitzer, Sulzberger, Katherine Graham, and Walter Lippman, the Maceys and Gimbels, Levi-Strauss, Ziegfeld and Schubert, David O. Selznick and the Warner Brothers, Paley and Sarnoff, Oppenheimer, Brandeis, and Einstein were all Jews, important, powerful, and above all, American.

Against these powerful American personalities of the Israelite persuasion Canadian Jewry can only offer the bootleg booze of the Bronfmans, the joyless McDonald's hamburgers of George Cohon (an American arriviste) and the Tallith tycoonery of the Reichman brothers. All these Jewish characters are marginal Canadian men; most lack entrée into Canadian high society; none had or have political power. Sam Bronfman couldn't even buy himself a senatorship. George Cohon is a Liberal but so far his Big Macs are a poor seller in the corridors of power. The skull caps of the Reichmans hide no kiss-curl-and-tell secrets of *real* political power.

All these Jews are neither real Americans nor mainstream Canadians. In fact, they and their fellow 300,000 Jews in Canada are strictly marginal Canadians at least as far as the WASP Canadian Boys in the Bland understand true Canadianism to be.

The Canadian Boys in the Bland's definition of true Canadianism was certainly not the same as the Jaded Observer's. When a tot, an adolescent, indeed even as an adult, the Jaded Observer was always asked his nationality. He always answered: "Jewish," not only because when he said "Canadian," he was always asked: "No! What are you really?" but because he knew Canadian meant Orange Lodge Anglo-Saxon and not Red Indian, High Anglican and not low Jew, surfboard not Serb, lacrosse not Lithuanian, Clark's pork and beans, not Hunky Bill's perogies, and above all, cute pug noses with freckles on them, and not magical false noses and glasses, magical in that the glasses came off but the noses didn't.

To the Jaded Observer, Canadian Jewish was really Jewish American north; Canadian also meant Uncle Ariah, the Miami Beach American Legionnaire, Uncle Lazer and his two New York communist sons hauled up for supposed treason before one Joe McCarthy. Canadianism meant loving Roosevelt, the CIO, Carol Lombard and the hot dog; it meant Hank Greenberg hitting fifty-eight home runs in one season and fellow Hebrew Sandy Koufax striking out more goyim than John L. Lewis. Being Canadian meant knowing that once Bess Myerson was Miss America in 1946, the Jaded Observer's sister-in-law could be the University of Alberta's first Jewish cheerleader, less than ten years later.

The Jaded Observer also knew that the George Grant-Margaret Atwood-Mel Watkins-Pierre Berton School of Canadian Navel Narcissism unconsciously, perhaps almost by accident, left the Jaded Observer out as the perpetual ethnic, always having to come in to the cold, cold Anglo climate of Anglo-Canadian nationalism. Like all other Canadian martians before him, the Jaded Observer also knew that Trudeau was a bit of a celestial spark, a quasi-friend, many times a fool and a fanatic anti-nationalist, but nevertheless one of the greats who, like the Jaded Observer, was not welcome to eat the fruit from the Atwood tree.

On all this Canadian Jewry often agreed with the Jaded Observer; often they too found the New Nationalism too bitter, too anti everything except fellow racial nationalists, be they Québécois, Vietcong, Sandinista or Palestinian. Jewish nationalism, i.e., Zionism, and the American nationalism of Vietnam-acid rain-candy floss-pay-TV were not the goodisms the New Canadian Nationalists were prepared to brew in their spiked cup of not-to-be-pitied all-Canadian tea.

Canadian nationalists tended to see Zionism as either Jewish imperialism or American imperialism masking itself in kibbutzism gear. American excesses in Vietnam were central to the renewal of Canadian nationalism. These excesses proved that if America's cultural thrust in Canada were not soon checked,

Canada too would be another Yankee-traduced Vietnam waste-
land. America's Vietnam nightmare made the Canadian nationalists' sales pitch an easy one.

The strident anti-Americanism of Canadian nationalism put it
on an inevitable collision course with Zionism, the excesses of
which much of Canadian nationalism's leadership, particularly
its Jewish leaders, soon began to deplore. Most of the Jewish
leadership in Canadian nationalism — Jim Laxer, Rick Salutin,
Cy Gonick, Abe Rotstein — were certainly taken aback by Israel's
ventures into Lebanon. Author Peter Newman and publisher Mel
Hurtig held their peace. The only prominent Canadian nationalist
to maintain the full Zionist line was Edwin Goodman, "Fast
Eddie" of Tory fame.

The full Zionist line, or even a fair portion of it, was embraced
by none of Canadian nationalism's non-Jewish leadership. There
was, of course, not the slightest scintilla of anti-Semitism or
Jewish self-hatred in all this, though many Canadian Jews and
non-Jewish spokesmen sadly rushed to those all too silly judge-
ments.

Canadian Jewry, whose passionate Zionism was only rivalled
by its exuberant Canadian patriotism, saw nothing wrong in its
Eddie Goodman-like love of both Canada and Israel. Rightly or
wrongly, Canadian Jewry saw no room for its split personality
in the New Canadian Nationalism of Grant-Watkins-Atwood.
The culture thrust of the American dream, not Canadian nationalism, seemed to offer Canadian Jewry the peaceable kingdom
they were so desperately searching for. The American dream,
after all, bought both Canadian patriotism and Zionism at a real
discount with no embarrassing questions asked. The New Canadian Nationalism, it seems, could only buy its own brand of
Canadian patriotism, and not the hybrid loyalties implicit in
Canadian Zionism.

Canadian Jewry, clinging from whatever rungs the Vertical
Mosaic allows some access to, or hiding under whatever Big
Mac branch plant gives them socio-economic shade, were prob-
ably first in the anglophone Canadian polity to shamelessly prefer

waving the American Manischewitz Matzoh ball wrapped in a Catskills borscht belt to saluting the Old Flag, wrapped around the Old Men forever preaching the Old Policies of Her Majesty's Britannic Canadians. Canadian Jews are also the only Canadians to prefer the soup of a chicken to the overbite of a beaver, the squeak of a poodle to the Baskerville bark of a labrador.

Certainly the Canadian Poles, despite the huge numbers of their relatives in Detroit, Buffalo, Milwaukee and Chicago, do not flaunt their American connection as Canadian Jews do. Not since the embarrassment of the Fenian Raids, the McGee assassination and the growth of the power of the Orange Lodges, have Irish Catholics in Canada reminded anyone of their shanty-and-lace-curtain Irish cousins in Boston or New York. Nor do Italian Canadians admit that Francis Ford Coppola's American Godfather vicariously atoned for them. For these ethnic Canadians, cellar dwelling in the Canadian mosaic is for the moment just fine, and Old Flag waving temporarily fulfilling, if not quite fun.

As for the Good True North Strong And Free Anglo-Saxon Canadian, he has been waving the Old Flag so long and so hard that he doesn't realize that culturally, ethnically and politically he himself is at best a branch plant Brit, at worst nothing but an old-fashioned colonel whimp; he is still living in Gunga Din sin with an Empire that no longer exists except under the iron heel of ruthlessness of its former Sabus turned ignoble savage. Today the sensitive tried and true Anglo-Canadian still gets his police, his firemen, his top military officers, his top theatre, radio and TV performers and producers, not to mention his journalists, from Great Britain's BBC and Fleet Street.

If Canadian Jewry truly loves Israel and is at least as American as Barney Miller and chopped liver, then WASP Canada is still as British as the red ensign (Ontario's very British official emblem and Dief's *idée fixe*) and more royalist than the Queen. Ethnic Canada may still be waving the Old Flag, buying the Old Policy and trusting any Old Man who's nice to them, and doing all of this out of ignorance and fear, but they have still seen Canadian Jews brazen out their American connection, and that lesson now observed will soon be learned — and not soon forgotten. Canadian Jewry can't help Americanizing Canada for Canadian Jewry simply loves America — its TV programs, its polyester suits, its "Jew Canoe" Cadillacs, its Catskill, Vegas and Miami Beach spas, its dirty movies and video discs, its kosher Chinese food, its stand-up comedians, its sex manuals and diet books, its five-toilet houses, its spectator sports. Even Canada's most important Rabbis — Fields, Plaut, Fineberg, Eisendrath, Aaron, Chiel, Frank, Rosenberg — are, or were, Americans who spent or spend their penal servitude in Canada, desperately trying to find out whether a Joe Clark or a George Hees is a Democrat or Republican, good or bad for the Jews and finally, if pushed hard enough, whether he's good or bad for Canada. The difference in gross Jewish vulgarity between Catskill Jewish loudmouths and those of the Laurentian Mountain variety has eluded the cultural morphologist Richler throughout a dozen books.

In this frank love of America, in this preference of Herman Wouk over Evelyn Waugh, of "Springtime for Hitler" over "Spring Thaw," of Rona Barrett over Zena Cherry, Canadian Jewry is frankly out of step with the New Canadian Culture of Atwood and Frye, the Old Canadian Culture of Front Page Challenge, and Berton to Kennedy to Sinclair to You. In this perpetually Fifties saga that is the New Canadian Nationalism, the central metaphor of American-Boy-Bully-Eats-Edible-Canadian-Girl-Innocent-Victim-Next-Door-Without-Really-Doing-Any-Bodily-Harm is one scenario in which the Chosen Few are definitely non-You. Instead Canadian Jewry is in bed with Bonzo and loving every perverted moment of it. The Canadian Jewish community wants the eyes of Texas to shine upon them; America's fiddlers dance on Forest Hill roofs; and Barbra Streisand, not Anne Murray, is Canadian Jewry's favourite Snowbird. At the very time the New Canadian Nationalism is very much old-fashioned Yankee baiting, Canadian Jewry is in the vanguard of preserving proletarian American culture in Canada. Like all vanguards, Canadian Jewry makes the natives restless.

Trudeau poses in the Supreme Court Chambers with his
appointee fresh from the Book of Judges, the first
Jewish chief justice of the Supreme Court, Bora Laskin.

Trudeau walks on the mild side with former principal secretary, Senator Jack Austin.

Austin brings to three the number of Jews sitting in the Trudeau cabinet. No other prime minister has been so comfortable with Jews; no other prime minister has been so uncomfortable — with Zionism and the policies of the State of Israel.

But the daughters of Judea had no better friend than Pierre Elliott Trudeau.

Owl Trudeau and the Pussycat at a United Jewish Appeal dinner in her honour, New York, 1983.

Trudeau and friends dance up a hora at Beth Zion Synagogue, Montreal, 1982. P.E.T.'s date for the evening was Melissa Singer-Cohn, second from right.

If Canadian nationalism were ever to take the down side of vicious racism, as Trudeau and Ramsay Cook have predicted, there will soon be a nativist Canada standing vanguard against the Canadian Jewish common carriers of the American cultural sickness. Canadian Jewry's love of America already carries with it the seeds of a possible bitter backlash. A poisonous 1984 broth of broken fiddles and spiked kreplach soup may just be ominously boiling away in the multicultural Canadian melting pot, as still another ethnic Canadian generation grows up anything but British prosaic, in the British Canadian-run mosaic.

Still, if Canadian Jewry is rubbing the New Canadian Nationalism raw, it has found cloying comfort and succulent succour in the ethnic drippings of the Canadian melting pot. For in Canadian ethnic land, the Jews are kings; the Italians, Portuguese, Greek, Chinese, and Slavic people who inhabit the basement apartments of the Vertical Mosaic look not to the WASPs but to Zion for social and economic guidance. The multiculturals admire the Jews who, not by deed, but by the example of their huge success in moving mosaics, provide them with their only spiritual guidance for survival in the Canadian WASP-made cultural rat race. The Canadian ethnic out to duplicate Jewish success seems determined to climb up every rung of Jacob's ladder, sure in the knowledge that once at the top he too will get his free lox and cream cheese on a bagel.

Trudeau, the Québécois PM, shared the Canadian Jewish love of America; it was American discos, films, TV programs, cowboy suits, American Jewish food and lifestyles that Trudeau saw duplicated around him everywhere in French Canada; it is a lifestyle that Trudeau himself enjoys; and above all it is a melting-pot style that melts down ethnic chauvinisms and nationalisms. Trudeau knew Colonel Sanders, McDonald's and Levi's were the three American horsemen of Quebec's national cultural apocalypse. Trudeau was equally aware that the more American the

Québécois became, the less separatist they would be. The more
the Yankee-style melting pot boils and bubbles in Quebec, the
less racist and the less chauvinist Quebec is bound to be. In the
battle for Quebec's soul, Trudeau's best soul brother was Uncle
Sam.

Uncle Sam always gave Trudeau more than an occasional help-
ing hand. Papa Trudeau was really nothing but an American-
style Québécois free enterprise Babbitt-booster. American boosterism had led Papa T. into the gas station business which was,
in retail, organizational and cultural terms, strictly American.
Finally, Papa Trudeau sold out to the Yankee Rockefellers for
a big-buck profit.

American boosterism made Pa Trudeau's Conservative politics
pro-business; naturally he favoured the politics of business boost-
ers Bennett and Duplessis. Philo-Americanism made Pa Trudeau
love American baseball and buy an American baseball farm team.
The Yankee itch to take a chance made both Pa and Pierre Trudeau
gamblers. Long before Trudeau had articulated his anti-nationalist views, his inherited love of America made him at worst a
continentalist, at best an internationalist. Trudeau's love of
America was easily equal to that of the Canadian Jews and the
Liberal Pearsonites.

Indeed so was Lévesque's philo-Americanism, but in the ardour
of René's Yankee love affair there was again a difference between
him and Trudeau. Trudeau's love of Americanism was his way
of showing the xenophobic French Canadian nationalists the
wonders and joys of the world's only proper and true internationalist society — America, America. When Trudeau squired
Barbra Streisand or some Texas beauty around, he was telling
insular Rimouski that the flesh-pots of Hollywood and Dallas
were theirs if only they'd smash their incubators of racist nationalism.

Lévesque used the American dream differently. It was the
Québécois love of America, Lévesque told his *sans culottes*, that
proved they were not anti-Anglo-Saxons but only against Anglo-
Canadians. Separatist love of America took separatism out of the

dangerous cauldrons of an anti-WASP racism, which the separatists really could not afford. Insularity, said René, was strength. Fortress America was the model for Fortress Quebec. The U.S. surely would not hate or tamper with a separate Quebec that loved it, even more than did Trudeau or Canadian Jewry. It is thus not surprising that the only world-class debate on Quebec separatism took place not in Canada but in the United States, with Trudeau wooing Washington and Lévesque wailing on Wall Street.

Unlike much of Anglo-Saxon Canada, both Trudeau and Lévesque always found themselves more at home in the United States than in the United Kingdom. For Lévesque, the U.K. was a symbol of his people's oppression and enforced inferiority. To Trudeau, the U.K. was somehow always the staunchest ally of his Anglo-Canadian Tory enemies. After all, it was not American congressmen, but British MPs and British high commissioners who tampered with his beloved constitution. (Trudeau hated them even more than the Gaullist French who meddled in Quebec and Canadian affairs.) Nor was it the Americans who created Ottawa's Oxford Old Boy Network, which Trudeau smashed wide open, using American university-trained Canadian Jewish boys to do it.

It is also America's melting pot, with its denial of legally-defined ethnicity and racial nationalism, that Trudeau's rationality has always passionately admired. Thus the American melting pot was really the model upon which multiculturalism was based, even though it was standard malpractice for Trudeau flaks and hacks to insist that multiculturalism was put in to keep the evil American melting pots away.

Multiculturalism came into being whether Trudeau liked it or not, because the French fact in Canada meant two nations, two official languages, two founding races — the full vocabulary and spirit of the ethnic chauvinism Trudeau had so often publicly challenged and denied. Thus, while the Official Languages Act in theory opened the joys and job rewards for bilingualism equally to everyone — Ukrainians and Unitarians, Macedonians and Moonies, Quakers and Québécois — it was the Québécois who were intended by Trudeau to mess with the pottage, patronage and plain good times all this brought. Trudeau's One Canada in effect meant two sets of superior beings — the Anglo-Saxons and the Frogs — at least as far as official and legalized ethnic and language status in Canada went. Bilingual Jews, Ukrainians, Poles and Laplanders could enjoy the thousand yaks that went with bilingual federal job service and were in no way discriminated against — except no one called them founding people or founding races. They were more the found-in people of Canada, people caught in the act of crapping out in the floating bilingualism game that was Trudeau's biggest gamble of all.

Having convinced himself that bilingualism would give his people the jobs and sense of personal worth they needed to assert French power without turning off the power current for the rest of the Canadian federation, Trudeau swallowed his anti-nationalist views and went ahead with Official Languages. Once that had created an inevitable void with Third Force Ethnic Canada, Trudeau stepped in with the band-aid of multiculturalism.

As mishmashes went, multiculturalism was pure political chopped liver. Having put two racial groups in a special status at the top of Jacob's ladder, Trudeau allowed the children of Jacob, Wasyl, White Feather, Atuk, Heinz and Bruno to fight unto death for supremacy on rung number three. Since not every group could win that neanderthal Darwinian race, Trudeau, the anti-ethnic nationalist, embraced the doctrine: "We are all ethnic but some of us are more ethnic than others. Henceforth all ethnics will be paid to be ethnic, particularly if you run ethnic newspapers and ethnic radio and TV stations which keep you ethnic and out of the Canadian mainstream of life where you would be at worst unwanted, and at best, uncomfortable."

In one fell swoop, Trudeau and multiculturalism had made third-class citizens out of a third of the country — that hitherto had felt only second-class. Wonder of wonders, distinguished rabbis, like the covenanter of Judaism, W. Gunther Plaut, embraced the new covenant-gospel of state-controlled, state-subsidized ethnicity. Canada's Jews, who got first star billing in the multicultural mosaic, played the Judas Goat to the other ethnics, who merrily rushed in to sacrifice the Anglo-Canadian heritage they had worked so hard to get, in order to keep the European and Asiatic heritages they had already enjoyed for centuries.

But the Jews were either too smart or too talented to forever slip down the slippery slope of multiculturalism. For Trudeau's One Canada in One Hundred Ethnic Parts to work, Trudeau needed the bilingual brains and talents of Canada's Jewish community. Under Trudeau, there were as many bilingual Jewish mandarins working the orange groves of Ottawa as there were Canadian Jewish-sponsored orange groves in Israel. Despite hints by Plaut and open assertions by the Jewish Defence League that Trudeau was a closet anti-Semite, P.E.T. had given the Jews more important and more numerous government and judicial jobs than all prime ministers before him combined.

Trudeau seems to have created a loophole in multiculturalism big enough for Canadian Jewry to walk through in droves. If Canadian Jewry could, so could other Canadian ethnic groups. Trudeau, king of the Francophones, was now also wearing the dubious new thornless crown of king of the Jews — and all other Canadian ethnics who dared to imitate the Chosen People. Now Jewish power given free rein by Trudeau even rivalled French power, not only on the banks of the Rideau but on the shores of the St. Lawrence, the Great Lakes and the great Pacific as well.

If anything, Trudeau was glad that the excellence of the Jews and the imitation of that excellence by other ethnic groups really made them all Canadians rather than "ethnics," and thus in essence rendered their multiculturalism component obsolete. Trudeau was only too glad to see multiculturalism melt down in a new thoroughly Canadian and exciting melting pot. To Trudeau, multiculturalism was now clearly less a war on the poverty of Canadian ethnic culture, but really a war on the poverty of Trudeau's own thoughts on federalism itself. In the beginning Trudeau knew that bilingualism and biculturalism needed multiculturalism to make the whole ethnic and racial mess that he had so far created a symmetrical mess at least.

Trudeau still hated ethnic nationalism as much as ever. But to outflank and isolate Quebec's separatism, not only was bilingualism and biculturalism necessary, but Quebec's ethnics had to be brought on side too. On behalf of Canadian ethnic solidarity with the state, Trudeau was prepared to drool over and finance the wonders of perogies, shish kebab, shashlik and kishka. Trudeau was even prepared to cast an indulgent eye up and down over Chinese characters and right to left for Hebrew and Yiddish ones and all around for the characters of the Cyrillic alphabet.

Trudeau was also aware that many ethnics in the mosaic were being subsidized to preserve cultures that regarded the pogrom as either rest and recreation or the normal hunting of Mr. and Mrs. Glass Under Tigers, cultures that kept women in the stone age and expressed political opinions ranging from Alaric the Vandal to Goering the Herman. That such racial and sexual chauvinism was being subsidized by a socialist-feminist Trudeau was one of the great Canadian ironies. These same ethnic groups often had a greater loyalty to a free Ukraine, Latvia, Lithuania and Estonia than to Canada and were, since the heyday of Diefenbaker's violent anti-communism, violently conservative; and from Day One virulently anti-Trudeau.

This aspect of multiculturalism had its piggy ironies too; Trudeau, the Cold War Dove, was subsidizing Canadian Ethnic Cold War Hawks at considerable expense to the taxpayers and at a considerable embarrassment to close Soviet-Canadian relations, which for Trudeau was always a top diplomatic priority. Trudeau, a Liberal, was subsidizing ethnic Tory voters; Trudeau, the rabid internationalist was propping up some of the most fanatic double-loyalty ethnic nationalists in the world. But, once he had embarked on multiculturalism, Trudeau had no choice but to live with these uninhabitables. At least he tried to starve multiculturalism for funds and provided it always with the weakest possible ministers.

Jewish refusal to stay within the ghetto walls of multiculturalism was welcomed by Trudeau. The involvement of the Jewish community's official leadership in multiculturalism, Trudeau also welcomed. Trudeau hoped traditional Jewish liberalism, scholarship and tolerance would make the multiculturalism pot less lumpen, less racist, or at least less ethnically nationalist.

Still there was a flaw in the ointment, a flaw Jewish Moral Majoritarian leaders like Emile Fackenheim and Gunther Plaut scratched at and irritated without ever understanding why or how. Trudeau loved Jews, individually and collectively, but as Canadian Jews, not as Zionists. The ethnicity of Zionism, and the potential of confused loyalties implicit in Zionism, irritated Trudeau, the disciple of the anti-nationalist Jews Kadourie and Kohn; Trudeau, the hater of FLQ terrorism, equally loathed the terrorism of Arafat and Irgun, and was uncomfortable with the excessive ethnicity of both the Palestinians and the Israelis.

Zionism made Trudeau edgy, unlike politicians Roy McMurtry or Jim Peterson, who were in Israel every other day making sure they could hang on to their Jewish constituencies. Trudeau visited Israel less than any other Western leader, and these visits never seemed to be top level affairs. Trudeau was also the first Canadian prime minister to pay a state visit to Saudi Arabia and North Yemen; the first prime minister to call for an independent Palestinian state and Israeli withdrawal from the West Bank. The brashness of Israel's clearly ethnic nationalism did not turn Trudeau on; neither did Arab jihadism.

Neither did the rather pushy, almost threatening, behaviour of Canadian Jewish leaders over Arab boycott legislation or moving embassies from Tel Aviv to Jerusalem make Trudeau do affirmative back flips. Trudeau refused to believe that Zionist lobbyists like London's Milton Harris, Montreal's Myer Bick or the Western Liberal Harold Buchwald spoke for H. Carl Goldenberg, Maxwell Cohen, Bora Laskin and Alan Gotlieb, Canadian Jews Trudeau had given important appointments to. They didn't, but they did speak for the vast majority of Canada's Jews, who see no incompatibility whatsoever between Liberalism, socialism, Canadianism and Zionism. Here Trudeau badly misread the Jewish community and lost at least two key Toronto Jewish seats in 1979 as a result.

Nor did the Last Days of Trudeau and their bunkerish behaviour help to unravel Trudeau-Jewish complications. Trudeau's apparent reversal of his own Mid-East policy, his condemnation of Israeli settlements on the West Bank, and his call for an independent Palestinian state, outraged the Canadian Jewish community and particularly those politicians — Jewish and Gentile — who represented Canadian Jewry. One Gentile Liberal MP was prepared to run for the Liberal leadership on the issue of Trudeau's Jewish betrayal; in caucus, bitter fights between Arabist and Zionist MPs and senators became a frequent occurrence. (At Trudeau's Last Supper in Toronto in mid-December 1983, the Jaded Observer noted only one picket group venting its spleen on Trudeau: the Canadian Jewish Defence League, demanding that the Defender of Canadian Jewry, In God's Name Go.)

But the Zionists misread Trudeau too. Far too many Zionists were ready to equate Trudeau's philosophical anti-Zionism with anti-Semitism. Here they were wrong. An overwhelming number of Canadian Jews knew that Trudeau was their best friend, the only Roosevelt they had or possibly would ever have.

Given men like Trudeau, Canadian Jewry knew that at last it could regard Canada as its own land of milk and honey. Given Trudeau's awesome respect for Jewish talent, Canadian Jews could for the first time in Canadian history begin to have respect for themselves and for what they could do for Canada. Given Canadian Jewish Uncle Tomism, flourishing as late as the mid-1960s, given the history since Confederation of Canadian Jewish wealth without equivalent Jewish power, Trudeau's opening of the floodgates of bureaucratic, political and judicial power to the Jews did not go unnoticed by most of Canadian Jewry.

Canadian Jews knew that Trudeau's less than enthusiastic espousal of Zionism was a philosophical deviation they would have to forgive him for. After all, they knew that Trudeau, the abstract theoretician, despised the separatists' flaunted affection for a France that had ignored Quebec for centuries, and that he had a basic contempt for the anglophone mania over royal weddings, tartans, welsh rarebits and cricket, too.

Canadian Jews understood the gut ethnic passions of the separatists and the Anglos because they felt these same passions for their fellow Jews in the United States, Israel and all over the world; still, as part of a people who had paid in holocaust currency for the excesses of nationalism, they not only shared but understood Trudeau's fears of nationalism's murky, shark-infested waters.

It was clear that, despite their differences, Trudeau and the Jews would always share a very special Canadian status. Trudeau was Lincoln, the Great Emancipator of Canadian Jewry, freeing them from the impotence of Uncle Tomism and the state denial of Jewish talent. Together, Trudeau and the Jews shared the special status of having melted down the Canadian mosaic and multiculturalism, Trudeau's own creation. In their love of Trudeau and before him, Laurier, the Canadian Jewish community had led English-speaking Canadians in the acceptance of French leaders and the French fact. In their steadfast social liberalism, Trudeau and the Jews had both helped to heal old wounds and exorcise old taboos. Trudeau had given Canadian Jewry not only equality but also its first taste of fraternity.

At last the Wandering Jews of Canada could put down their walking sticks and knapsacks and rest awhile. Next year, they might be in Jerusalem, but for most Canadian Jews, because of Trudeau this year, next year, next century, it was Canada, O Canada, Oi Vey all the way.

6 Succession Duties

Shortly after Trudeau's cliff-hanging survival act of 1972 had become official, the Jaded Observer, live in front of millions, was asked by a breathless Lloyd Robertson: "What does the future hold for Pierre Elliott Trudeau?" "Everything," the Jaded Observer answered blithely, "but only if Trudeau, the Philosopher King, becomes Mackenzie King." That phrase has since lived in infamy but the transition it invoked never did quite come about. Being a philosopher king or a Mackenzie King is not an addiction easily disposed of. To get rid of philosopher kings you force-feed them hemlock; to get rid of a Mackenzie King you can rely only on the ravages of senility. (Even then you're not sure; it was months after St. Laurent was chosen leader before the rapidly aging King gave up the prime ministership, an act he regretted privately until his dying day.)

Trudeau after 1972 never quite abdicated the kingship of the philosopher nor did he fully embrace the tricks of the Mackenzie Kingship. From 1972 to 1979 Trudeau remained a political hermaphrodite, with half the political organs of a Lyceum licentiate and half the sensory antennae of Wee Willy King. Trudeau's new political personality was far more schizophrenic than harmonious.

In 1979, seven years into his Mackenzie Kingship, Trudeau suffered his only election loss. Rather than take up the challenging role of Leader of the Opposition, a role with no bureaucratic, administrative or intellectual inputs, a role strictly political and Mackenzie Kingish, Trudeau resigned instantly and went into exile.

This kind of face-saving retreat and defeatism philosopher kings rarely engage in, and Mackenzie Kings never do. The defeated philosopher king simply moves to another park bench in the Lyceum, and his soliloquies brilliantly rationalize away the slings and arrows of his recent sorrows. Mackenzie King's defeats — one constitutional in 1926, one electoral in 1930 — were in an odd way joyously embraced, for as a parliamentarian few could equal Mackenzie King in opposition. Only there could King be the complete politician, untrammelled by bureaucratic or policy demands. The professional Philosopher King and the politician Mackenzie King both realized opposition was a refurbishing, revitalizing process and the only beachhead really left for the recovery of power. Trudeau's seeming incapacity to grasp the joys of defeat, to live with defeat as so many millions of Canadians have to do daily, certainly did much to take the magus-magic-mickey out of his relationship with the Canadian people. Canadians do not quite trust a magician-politician who cannot compromise, who cannot ever saw his loved ones, his party or his country in half. This seeming moral ambivalence, perhaps moral cowardice, set Trudeau apart not only from philosopher kings and Mackenzie Kings but from the proper exercise of leadership itself. It was just-watch-me, thumb-in-the-mouth politics at a very sad, dysfunctional level.

Clearly it was not the drive of character, the call of the wild or charisma magnetics that finally rescued Trudeau from political oblivion in 1980; the purest of pure luck, not cunning, nor the a priori tricks of the Kantian philosopher, brought Trudeau back from oblivion.

Bad luck and pure hate — the hate of the unemployed for a leader who thumbed his nose at their despair; the hate of an Anglo-Saxon Canada convinced that Trudeau and his francophones had unfairly displaced them; the hate of the most cozzened and privileged business class in the country's history convinced that sooner or later Trudeau and his bureaucrats would puncture their bloated balloon; the hate of the Beautiful People convinced that Trudeau's boring administrative and bureaucratic style of government was not of the swinger they had once loved and cherished...these things and these things alone — finally drove Trudeau from office.

In that sense too Trudeau is unique. No philosopher king and no Mackenzie King was ever hated by so many Canadians for so many different reasons. King was only hated by British Canadians for his conscription military policies, was at least tolerated by the French Canadians, the ethnics, the labour leaders and the Western and Ontario farmers who constituted the key elements of his coalition. The confrontationist Trudeau, in Quebec, created a sufficient backlash all by himself to virtually elect the first Quebec separatist government. Trudeau's wage and price controls earned him the undying enmity of organized labour. Trudeau's intellectual and city-slicker ways drove the rustics to demonic distraction. Trudeau's willingness to parlay with Moscow or the Palestinian Liberation Organization earned him the bitter loathing and contempt of large numbers of Canadian ethnics.

Indeed the one thing Trudeau's confrontation politics bred was the sound and fury of outraged reaction. Pearson's "politics of joy" had with Trudeau become the War of Words, the angry denunciations and bitter recriminations of a Canada in perpetual verbal combat. Inevitably the politics of confrontation began to breed countervailing responses — the politics of quietism and retrenchment, of conspicuous consumption, of more take than give, of human rights over old freedoms, of affirmative action for many haves and affirmative restraint for most have-nots.

This trendy, sophisticated neo-conservatism was a kind of adulterated sweetness and light: not the sweetness and light of Matthew Arnold but the simplistic political rhythms of the Harding that followed Wilson and the "Ike" that followed Truman. The suburban and boonie Babbitts soon began to rattle and roll the Trudeau throne; the cry for "normalcy" was now strident, vicious and loud. The land was now saccharin and eagerly awaiting the sweet smell of succession.

It is this succession that was perhaps Trudeau's most bizarre gift of all. For one thing it was the first Liberal succession in Canadian history that was not from Father to Son or a benevolent neutrality emanating from Father to All My Sons. Laurier did not live long enough to choose his own successor, but few spoke as eloquently for the Laurier heritage as Mackenzie King. The orchestration of St. Laurent's nomination by King was worthy of Barnum, full of fake leadership races by prominent cabinet ministers like C. D. Howe and Doug Abbott playing stalking-horses for Uncle Louie, full of threats of denied senatorships and judgeships, but refreshingly free of any perplexities, ambiguities or organizational confusion.

Pearson's anointment was even simpler. His apparent neutrality in 1968 was conveniently synchronized with the Trudeau bandwagon. Only the blind and the obtuse could conclude that the Pearson choice was a sacerdotal mystery.

But the Trudeau succession was to be another matter. It would, of course, be silly to suggest that Trudeau had a cyclops eye out for Turner. Turner's sins were quite apparent. In all the years that Turner had served ably in Trudeau's administration, he was always best known for being the only real leader of Trudeau's opposition. In cabinet Turner pushed the views of business, Trudeau the macho-bureaucratic views being daily generated by the PMO/PCO. Turner led by the act of adroit followership, by consensus, by the slap on the back, the crook of the knee or the carefully planted tickle. Turner believed in quietism, not Trudeau activism; Turner believed in jockstrap intimacies exchanged by business leaders, government leaders and labour leaders, in private.

Turner respected kingship but not philosopher-kingship, for to Turner a king without a defined territory was simply a mouthpiece for himself. But above all, Turner distrusted intellectuality. As a perpetual pragmatist, Turner wished to test his ideas only in the real marketplace; there he was convinced his ideas would be safer and more secure. Testing ideas in dialectic forms, in front of philosopher kings to see what *dang an sichs*, Kantian things in themselves, would ultimately pop up, was a behaviour pattern of Trudeau's that either annoyed or terrified Turner.

Trudeau's aversion to Turner was obviously simple enough. Jock or sports-metaphor politics were anathema to Trudeau. As a just-watch-me politician, Trudeau was first comfortable primarily among his own people, the people who most enjoyed watching him; rarely did Trudeau have English or even Jewish cronies. P.E.T.'s best buddies — Jean LeMoyne, Jacques Hébert, Gérard Pelletier, Jean Marchand — he put in the Senate or in ambassadorships, as with Pelletier. With the exception of Marchand, Trudeau's cronies were always intellectuals, and rarely businessmen. Trudeau was comfortable with a Senator Ian Sinclair of the CPR or a Paul Desmarais, but these gentlemen were hardly intimates. Trudeau certainly disliked Turner's pro-business sympathies and his philosophy of political quietism; he found Turner shallow and his pragmatism often bordering on moral cowardice.

Presumably Trudeau, the socialist stranger to Liberalism, was pleased to see that he was far better liked at the leadership convention than the exile Turner who had just come in from the cold. Trudeau was visibly pleasured by the desperate sycophancy with which Turner had come to the convention to praise him.

Trudeau, who revelled in his brief hostile encounters with the press, surely regarded Turner's assiduous wooing of the same with some contempt. Always more Trudeau than Elliott, the Prime Minister saw himself as a man with fixed Quebec roots, and Turner as a sort of Canadian Wandering Jew — today Vancouver, tomorrow Quebec, the day after, Ottawa, the day after that, Toronto. Trudeau the hard-core federalist found it easy to tell himself that Turner's pragmatism could only lead to Two Nations. Lévesque's instant confirmation of Turner's Manitoba language policy during the leadership campaign certainly speeded up such a Trudeau thought process. Finally, Trudeau was aware that Turner had led the anti-Trudeau forces in Canada, and P.E.T. couldn't help but notice that the corporate world had rallied to Turner's cause every mammonite convinced that Trudeau had personally denied him an investment benefit, a tax write-off, a subsidy.

But if Trudeau knew his enemy he did precious little to fight him. In 1984, as the polls plunged, as the sands of Peace In Our Time ran out, as Trudeauphobia was the only bit of political culture that most Canadians shared, Trudeau's political stance was still My Way All The Way. As in 1979 and 1980, Trudeau in 1984 was still doing his "If I am called I shall serve again" number; as always Trudeau made it clear that he preferred the miseries of an Edwardian abdication to the holocaust of Napoleonic defeat.

Trudeau did little to connive to hang on to the Liberal leadership. Nor did he ever split his party on racial and cultural lines as his Conservative opponents seemed to do so effortlessly. Trudeau accepted the massive affections and plaudits of the 1984 Liberal convention, but he did warn of his own succession duty: he would be keeping a watching brief on Turner's disposal of the Trudeau reform legacy. There would be no more Trudeaus to kick around; but there would still be a Trudeau to drop kick the odd fool.

Still, Trudeau had tiptoed unobtrusively into the quiet of the night. The gunslinger had not died with his boots on, nor was he exactly barefoot in the park. Trudeau, it seems, would have to look out for his heritage — all by himself. He had left few chits behind for anyone to cash in: certainly none for Turner; few if any for Jean Chrétien; and not that many for Jim Coutts, that loyal cherub of malice, that winged messenger bearing Trudeau's greeting cards. Coutts may have been Trudeau's Hermes, perhaps his Caliban, but certainly not his close friend or crony.

As for Lady Iona, beauteous as she is, there was no key there to unlock Trudeau's Excalibur. Perhaps this was because Iona was fond of telling the media that, given three months, she could pick up economics and be as fluent in that "dismal science" as her prime minister, a lifetime student of the subject; or because there was virtually zero in the way of animal magnetism between Lady Iona and King Arthur Pierre. Iona's failure to turn on either the Philosopher King or the Mackenzie King in Trudeau, or to reach him either intellectually or playfully, was no bar to her membership in cabinet or to the party presidency. But it must have had something to do with Trudeau's failure to take either her real bid for a senatorship and her apparent bid for Liberal leadership seriously. Iona's power, like Flora's before her, Trudeau was certain, would be a blooming thing going into a convention but a wilting one going out.

Trudeau the meritocrat did argue against the iniquities of the Liberal leadership alternation myth. Only the best man, French or English, should be chosen, Trudeau carefully insisted (a titch more carefully than when Pearson made similar denials in 1968). Certainly Jean Chrétien was not in 1984 Trudeau's man. In 1968 Chrétien was the only Quebec minister not to support Trudeau. Chrétien, the darling of the press, the Beautiful People and what passes for populism in the Liberal Party, in 1968 shared Mitchell Sharp's and the financial community's opinion that Trudeau was somehow still too radical for traditional Canadian Liberalism.

Chrétien's contacts in the business community have always been good. Liberal Party bagmen, oil and gas lobbyists, Bay Street honchos, Big Blue Machiners like Ontario Attorney General Roy McMurtry, have always enjoyed Chrétien's Poor Johnny jokes and his evocation of the People, because they are sure that Chrétien cannot raise the People out of their torpor, and even if Chrétien could, he would divert the People's energies into safe channels. The Chrétien campaign was run by his former executive assistant, Johnny Rae, now a president of a Desmarais company. Chrétien's daughter is married to Desmarais's son. Mitchell Sharp, still the one ex-bureaucrat-politician Big Business really trusts, always has the ear of Jean Chrétien. Compared to Trudeau, Chrétien is as radical as Mrs. Wiggs and the marketplace of his ideas as different and varied as her Cabbage Patch. Chrétien's intellectuality even suffers by comparison to Turner, and it is an aspect of Chrétien that has made at least intellectual intimacy with Trudeau virtually impossible.

Nor was social bonding with Chrétien easy for Trudeau. The son of the Shawinigan sawmill and the Outremont salon socialist had little in common except their love of One Canada. Trudeau prided himself on a reason, cold and steely; Chrétien on a passion,

Trudeau greets John Turner, the man from Glad Hand, just after naming him finance minister in 1972.

Trudeau pays his succession duties by remaining silent about his successor; but Turner's corporate image, cautious politics and Babbitt ideology appeal to neither the Philosopher King nor the Mackenzie King in Trudeau.

Paying the succession duties for Jean Chrétien is even trickier for Trudeau.

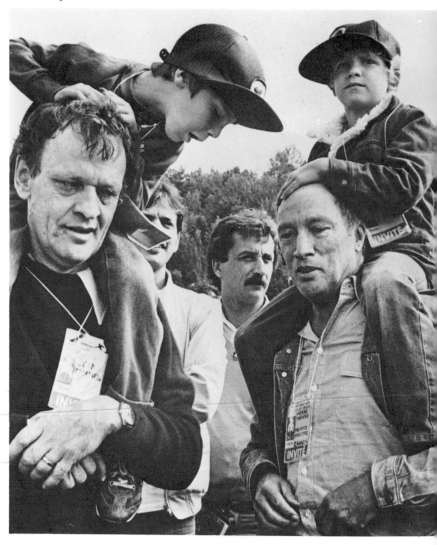

Chrétien is the one Quebec minister who did not support him for the leadership in 1968. Trudeau remains silent but his mantle does not quite cover the Man from Shawinigan.

The candidate who might have received Trudeau's blessing was Marc Lalonde, his oldest and most faithful servant.

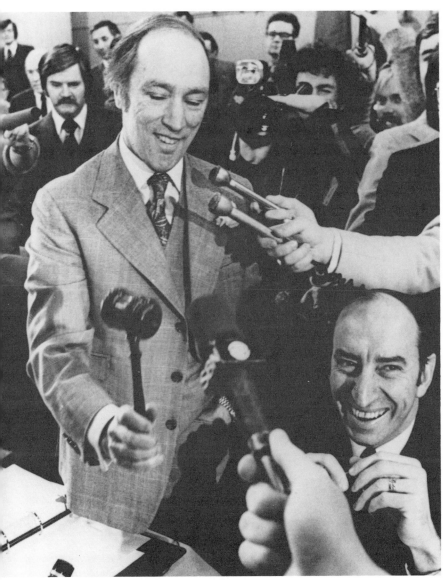

But Lalonde believed in alternating English and French leaders — almost as much as Trudeau did in 1968.

Trudeau and Lévesque — the I'm okay, you're okay of Quebec politics.

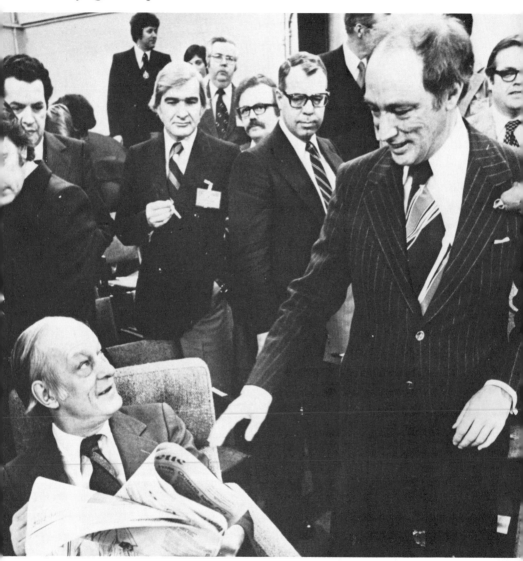

This is the toughest succession duty of all: had Trudeau failed in Quebec, the federalist option would have failed with him.

fiery and demagogic. The elitist Trudeau had little respect for the antithesis of elitism — the cult of populism so expertly practised by Chrétien. Trudeau saw himself as the inheritor of the aristocratic, knightly Liberalism of Laurier and St. Laurent. He could only look askance at a Chrétien Liberalism uncomfortably close to the populist demagoguery of a Duplessis, a Hepburn, a Wacky Bennett.

Trudeau, who hated both Big Business's manipulation of politics and the populists' inflaming of the passions, could see little in the way of a successor in Chrétien, and more of a threat to the integrity of his reasoned Liberal legacy. Trudeau the intellectual, the snob, would never put his mantle on the broad proletarian shoulders of the Shawinigan Man. Trudeau the upper-class perfectionist was always uncomfortable with a Chrétien who seemed to be bringing back to Canadian politics a pea souper-habitant motif last seen with Réal Caouette. Kings never anoint peasants; philosopher kings like Trudeau do not have dynastic dealings with proletarians like Chrétien.

The value of choosing your own successor, your own son for the family business, your own daughter for Hollywood stardom, is that the process spells continuity, implies life after death, and above all, the taking on by safe hands of the work you've not yet finished. The absence of a carefully planned, stylistically orchestrated Trudeau laying-on-of-hands and passing-on-of-the-ring raises some interesting questions. Does it suggest that Trudeau feels his work has been done, is complete and symmetrical and need not be handed over to anyone?

Probably not. Self-assured as Trudeau may be, he could not have helped but realize how fragile his legacy is. If the domestic peace of bilingualism and biculturalism could be shattered by the slightest Turnerian remark, then the house of Two Solitudes could as easily be huffed and puffed down by any Trudeau successor whose psychic feel for Quebec and its nuances was not quite that of Pierre Elliott Trudeau. The peace posture of a philosopher king could most easily disappear in a new Canadian foreign policy redolent of Mackenzie King isolationism. The country's cultural industries might find it difficult to rationalize their existence before a new prime minister who thinks culture can only come from the barrels of corporate fast guns.

But above all, succession duties in Liberal politics imply that every Liberal leader has a natural successor; or at least they do in Liberal mythology. Mackenzie King may have had to withstand the shrewish devices of Lady Laurier, but in 1919 King, friend of business, labour and the francophone, was the only natural successor to Laurier. St. Laurent was certainly King's only natural successor. Compared to the variety of riches and talent in the francophone division of Trudeau's cabinet, King's francophone contingents were invariably unilingual, poorly educated and completely unsuitable as prime ministerial material. Ernest Lapointe and Louis St. Laurent were the only two exceptions and Lapointe died before King could anoint him. King's determination to start the alternation theory left him with St. Laurent as the one and only natural successor.

In 1958 Pearson was the one man the Liberals could turn to and still keep a straight face. Those Liberals who could not keep a straight face knew Pearson faced many years in opposition as the Diefenbaker juggernaut, having surprised the Liberals in 1957, was soon to annihilate them in 1958. Pearson, as successors go, was a definite natural; he was the only natural leader, ready, aye, ready and willing to be the sacrificial lamb.

But above all, Trudeau was the natural successor to Pearson. Lester Bowles Pearson himself acknowledged Trudeau's superiority over the Pearson ragtag, piecemealymouth compromise school of government. Trudeau clearly promised challenge, action, commitment and above all things, the changing of the guard, the ringing in of the final changes on the past, and the boastful assumption that the future could be changed now, before anyone knew exactly what it was, for if not acted upon now it would surely change us before we changed it.

In 1968 even Liberal reactionaries favoured progress. Change for the sake of change became the catchword, the *raison d'être*, for everything that moved in the Liberal Party in 1968, even for mocked Liberal turtles like Paul Martin, Paul Hellyer and Bob Winters, who still wished to crawl along the sands of time. In 1968 even the most conservative of Conservatives, never mind Liberals, had bought Expoism, the philosophy that told us: today exhibit the talents of the world, tomorrow possess them.

In 1968 Trudeau, the master quick change artist of all time, was supported by the bulk of Canada, which shared his conviction that change even for the sake of change is better than treading windmills or slowly sucking wind. By 1984 the speed and volume of Trudeau's legislative reforms were unequalled in Canadian history; unequalled too was the vacuum of leadership Trudeau had left behind. Trudeau had tackled every major controversial problem facing the nation. Apparent legislative handles had been fixed on this shopping bag of goodies: homosexuality, apprehended insurrection, official languages, inflation, price and wage controls, and a Canadian constitution. PetroCan had been set up, a national energy policy launched, foreign ownership reviewed if not curtailed, cultural industries protected from Yankee competition, peacemaking converted into a permanent global operation, the defence establishment curbed, Senate reforms proposed, party financing legalized.

If legislative enactments are to be trusted, if state public relations hoopla and manipulation is to be given a semblance of credibility, if executive skills channelled into legislative outputs earn a proper cluck, cluck of approval, then P.E.T. is the greatest lawmaker we have ever had, indeed the only Solon to grace our shores. The Trudeau legislative thrust easily outweighed the accomplishments of all legislators, cabinet ministers and mandarins who tended the grapes of wrath for Canada in the innocent years 1867 to 1967 combined.

Accomplishment on this scale inevitably rules out successors both natural or otherwise. All that followed Trudeau is pure followership itself, the best of the boys available for a job no one can fill — at least not as well as Trudeau. The succession duties of P.E.T. are costly, indeed prohibitive. Neither the Liberal Party nor John Turner can really pay them.

This style of succession created a huge vacuum into which Liberal leadership aspirants tumbled at their peril. Since not one of these aspirants could fill Trudeau's shoes in 1984, each was a simple anti-climax in search of a proper place to record his non-fulfillment. The vacuum was so ominous, and the living Trudeau looked so good compared to the Liberal Lilliputians clinging to his ankles, that the potential successors were made to feel small and to look impotent. The new leader would have to fight not only the reality of Mulroney and the Tories but the bigger reality of the incorruptible Pierre. Canadians could and did ask themselves this question: Can a party that wants Trudeau to go and Chrétien-Turner-Roberts-Coutts-Munro to stay really deserve anyone's vote?

The Liberal Party has been left by Trudeau in a state somewhere between anorexia and asphyxia. Canadian political parties can only flourish in a parliamentary, not a presidential, atmosphere. Trudeau's presidential politics reduced the Liberal Party to the Democratic Party North — dead from the waist up for four to five years, then massaged at election time from the waist down into sudden quickened, if erratic, behaviour. The well-oiled party machine of Mackenzie King, despite that watcher of the dead's shrouded aura of command, always delivered, even though mostly from behind. An effective Liberal Party saved St. Laurent from total rout in 1957 and took a diplomatic pantywaist like Pearson to heights undreamt of even in the parsonage. After P.E.T., after his just-watch-me, my-way presidential politics, the Trudeau Liberal Party is virtually a hollow shell, a figment of the imaginations of Davey, Coutts and Goldfarb. The Trudeau Liberal Party can no longer deliver anyone, nor is the new Turner Liberal Party asking the Trudeauites to come aboard.

John Turner is certainly not a figment of the imagination; rather he is a figment Liberal, a man so truncated from the mainstream of Trudeauism that he has virtually created his own party — the Bay Street-Main Street, the glad-hand in the '50s handshake, the joys of jockdom, the rock rock rock of turning the clock clock clock back back back, the cosmology of status quo ante, the ante of two steps backward to every step forward, the passing of the torch to the Babbitts and plutocrats, the lighting of your communal bonfires by the light beams of the silvery moon.

Like Trudeau, Turner has stolen the Liberal Party for himself. And like Trudeau, he will not return it intact. Trudeau infused the Liberal Party with his "do-goodism," if you like, his socialism. The plans John Turner has for the Liberal Party are quite different: the only succession duties Turner is willing to pay for are the six silver nails he plans to drive into Trudeau's political coffin. The consensual Turner promises his party the joyous return to King-St. Laurent days. It is this implicit promise with which Turner beguiled friendly, greedy delegates at the Liberal convention. Rusty Turner may have been; in this delicate, yet lucrative, sphere Turner hit many nails on the head.

In this game of who's got Liberalism where, Chrétien was also out to lunch. Chrétien's contacts and rapport with Trudeau or even Davey and Coutts were minimal. Unlike Turner, he had no base with the Trudeau oppositionists who bulked large in the party apparatus and at the convention. While Turner hobnobbed with the senators and provincial presidents who ran the Liberal Party, Chrétien relied on the considerable skills of past and present executive assistants like John Rae or Eddie Goldenberg, who still had little, if any, contact with the real Liberal Party machine. A Chrétien victory over the Liberal Party in effect had to be quite like Trudeau's: the Canadian public, particularly the radical chichi and Beautiful People, would have to thrust Chrétien onto a basically English party he little understood. In 1968, Trudeau's ignorance of English Canada was disguised by his fluent bilingualism and biculturalism. Chrétien's French unilingualism shut him out of English Canada until the early 1970s, when he immersed himself in English language courses. (Frequently Chrétien would ask Anthony Westell of the *Toronto Star* and the Jaded Observer if they could lunch with him so he could practise the Queen's English.) But today Chrétien's grasp of and rapport with English Canada is probably less than Trudeau's was in 1968.

If in 1968 Trudeau was in large part hand-delivered to the

Liberal Party, there seemed to be little, if any, pushing back by the Liberals. Soon the Liberals swallowed Trudeau's activism, his socialism, as if that was the elixir they had been thirsting for all their political lives. Trudeau became quickly not only the man who came to Grit dinner but the man who dined on the Liberal Party. In 1984 the Liberal Party was pure and simply — Trudeau; Trudeau's succession, not Trudeau's abdication, was the real act of *lèse-majesté*.

Trudeau the Incorruptible, it now seems, had become Trudeau the Irreplaceable; the duty to succeed him had now become the Impossible Dream. Still, the self-respecting observer, the popular historian, owes these dialectic duties if not to the Trudeau succession, then to the Trudeau record, the Trudeau *Zeitgeist*.

Pierre Elliott Trudeau neither discovered nor nurtured the idea of a single Canada. Trudeau's Canadas were as numerous as the sands on the seashore, or the multicultural grants or the designated bilingual jobs so freely dispensed by his government. Diefenbaker had left the beginnings of a viable melting pot in his One Canada. Trudeau replaced that with a One Canada of many tongues: vanishing tongues pickled in portentous chauvinism like Latvian, Estonian and Yiddish, preserved by the Berlitz walls of the Trudeau state; the Master Mother Tongues of English and French, which mastered together got the Canadian upper-middle classes the best of bureaucratic bonbons; and the rhetoric-ridden tongues of politicians who insisted that all this in no way harmed anyone. Trudeau was not the father of One Canada, he was the successful developer, architect and town planner of Babel Towers Canada, a vertically mosaicked condominium complex where no one put up and no one ever shut up.

Nor was Trudeau totally a bloody-minded single-combat warrior, a crazed Napoleon-gunslinger in search of internal and domestic violence to quell. The War Measures crisis was not the supine cave-in to imminent fascist instincts that Canadian civil libertarians so love to see cropping up everywhere. True, it was just-watch-me politics in which Mr. Living History Himself thrived, but his reasoning on the subject was shared, and is still

What endures of the Trudeau record is more than mere legislation, more than innovation or change for the sake of change. What's left is a man of passion...

A man of the people...

A superb parliamentarian...

The pirouette in power...

The Clown Prince...

The Canadian Gothic King...

The sybarite . . .

The father who knows best...

The Godfather who does too...

The man of solitude...

And one Canadian who will never fade into the sunset.

shared, by the most rational slice of the Canadian political community. True, the radical chichi, the Beautiful People of Toronto, maintain their splendid isolation on the subject. Arguments about War Measures still breed excess on all sides. Those who found Trudeau too slow to invoke the national emergency were just as appalled as those who found the proclamation too quick and too severe. Still, the Trudeau succession works and history comes full circle. *Saturday Night*, which could never find it in its collective heart to forgive Trudeau, has instead, in a splendidly sensitive cover story, forgiven convicted FLQ kidnapper Paul Rose.

Nor was Trudeau ever the Machiavellian of populist and radical chic folklore. Diefenbaker was always fond of noting that the Penguin edition of *The Prince* had a cover portrait of Machiavelli which resembled Trudeau to a T. Diefenbaker often showed the Jaded Observer this picture but the Observer did not have the heart to tell the Chief that this penguin face also looked a great deal like Israel Asper, former Liberal leader in Manitoba, Peter Kent of CBC's ''The Journal'' and Art Eggleton, mayor of Toronto.

Trudeau was certainly a titch shrewd in his handling of the Chief. The more Diefenbaker quarrelled with Stanfield the more Trudeau would tell people at Ottawa's chichi parties that ''I just love that man.'' Not even Diefenbaker's hostility to the Official Languages Act could cool the ardour of Trudeau's affections. Diefenbaker was given one of the best offices on Parliament Hill, right across from Stanfield's, so Diefenbaker could properly spook the Nova Scotian (Trudeau even installed a shower room in Diefenbaker's office so that the Chief could daily scrub off his deadly sins).

But all this is not Machiavellian. When it came to reading Tory strategy on something as controversial as official languages, Trudeau was more a gullible Gulliver than a Medici manoeuvrer. Trudeau was for months convinced that Peter Reilly, the angry Tory MP from Ottawa West, was a virulent anti-Frog. When the Jaded Observer told Trudeau one day that Reilly had that very morning given the best speech yet heard in the House in favour of Official Languages, Trudeau was stunned but quite grateful. Nor was Trudeau's 1984 resolution on Manitoba's bilingualism intended to trap novice parliamentarian Mulroney. Trudeau generally felt the country was drifting away from the bilingualism commitment. Turner proved him right. Trudeau was always a clever leader; Trudeau was never an amoral one.

Nor was Trudeau a master of Quebec politics. In many ways Trudeau was pure Mackenzie King. Lapointe ran Quebec for King, Lalonde ran Quebec for the Philosopher King. Indeed a great deal of what strength Trudeau had in Quebec came vicariously. Seeing Trudeau's mastery over the elites of English Canada, Quebec felt relieved enough to flirt with the separatism of Lévesque. A weak Trudeau in Quebec would have meant the virtual end of Canadian federalism by now. Trudeau was master of Quebec far more than he was master in Quebec; Lévesque's position is almost the vice versa.

If Trudeau really wasn't a master politician in the traditional sense, even in Quebec, then the succession he leaves behind there is tricky. Trudeau did not groom a proper federalist leader of the province of Quebec. If Lalonde was such a leader, he'd have been in the leadership race. Chrétien's grasp of the Quebec machine was equally dubious. The best arrangement Turner will come to in Quebec will be a Mackenzie King one; Turner will silently surrender the Quebec job to someone else. Ironically Trudeau's One Canada disciple, Brian Mulroney, is the one Canadian politician with the best skills for becoming the next master of the Quebec House. Certainly Mulroney is as much of Quebec and of Trudeau as either Chrétien or Lalonde, and in some circumstances could keep the Trudeau bunting flying high in Quebec.

Certainly in that result would be the oddest Trudeau succession duty the Canadian people would have to pay. By now most fair-minded Canadians have paid or are paying off the succession duties of Pierre Elliott Trudeau. Above all, Canadians must learn to assess and review the Trudeau record with the objectivity

Trudeau's startling accomplishments deserve. Trudeau must not be allowed to fall into the hands of the instant revisionists before he has had a fair chance to judge Himself. Being Trudeau he may choose silence. In that case, Canadians must speak up for him. The one Trudeau succession duty still outstanding is this: let us judge ourselves first before we judge Himself, for so much of Himself is really ourselves.

One last thought:

The Trudeau giant is in the tree, and the less than radical Jacks are in charge of the Liberal beanstalk. The native dancers are back on the marathon dance floor. Trendy Trudeau is scattering his epaulettes everywhere. The band is about to play his song — the Dance of the Dialectic — again. The ex-philosopher king, the once Mackenzie King knows all the steps to this one — one step backwards and two steps forward. Trudeau plans to add new dancers to the repertoire — the Incorruptible Elder Statesman, the Professional Gadfly, the Senior Spoil-sport, the Raunchy Revisionist.

The game is not yet over. Nor is the game the same. But the Trudeau message is: Carry on without me, Canada — if you can!

June 14, 1984.

Dance of the Dialectic
Larry Zolf
Dance of the Dialectic is a stunning *tour de force*, the story of
Canadian politics from 1968 to 1973 and an account of how Pierre
Elliott Trudeau's government and the Ottawa press gallery together
made and re-made the political mood of the country. "It's the
funniest and truest book I've read this year" — Allan Fother-
ingham, syndicated columnist.

The Asbestos Strike
Edited by Pierre Elliott Trudeau
Pierre Elliott Trudeau first came to prominence with this classic
study of the Asbestos strike of 1949, published originally in French
as *La Grève de l'amiante*. As Trudeau wrote, the struggle between
asbestos miners and the united forces of the mining companies
and the Duplessis government was "a turning point in the entire
religious, political, social and economic history of Quebec."
"An exceptionally able analysis...Trudeau's opening chapter
remains as brilliant as ever." — Ramsay Cook, *Canadian Forum*.

The Liberal Idea of Canada
Pierre Trudeau and the Question of Canada's Survival
James Laxer & Robert Laxer
This trenchant study examines the Trudeau regime, Trudeau's
efforts to modify the system of ideology and policy he inherited

in 1968, and the prolonged effects Trudeau's liberalism has had on the country.

"An essential resource for a cogent discussion of where we are and how we got here." — Dalton Camp.

The Age of Mackenzie King
Henry Ferns and Bernard Ostry

This witty and perceptive study of Mackenzie King's career up to 1919 was first published in 1955. Its critical attitude to King earned it little favour in that day, but since being republished in 1976 it has become widely regarded as a remarkable book well ahead of its time.

"Ferns and Ostry have pinned down their victim like a prize butterfly." — Peter C. Newman.

Willie: *A Romance*
Heather Robertson

Willie: A Romance is a rollicking historical novel centred around one William Lyon Mackenzie King during the years of the Great War. Winner of the 1983 *Books in Canada* First Novel Award, *Willie* has been acclaimed from coast to coast.

"A bravura performance, bursting with creative energy...a triumph." — William French, *Globe and Mail*.

Brian Mulroney
The Boy from Baie-Comeau
Rae Murphy, Robert Chodos and Nick Auf der Maur

This new book presents the complete story of Brian Mulroney's life in business and politics. The goal of the Tory leadership was one "the boy from Baie-Comeau" had early, and he pursued it with a vengeance through a meteoric law career, as an unswerving wheelhorse for the Conservative cause in Quebec, and in the five-year stint as president of the Iron Ore Company of Canada. "Lively, readable, perceptive...brought skillfully together." — Montreal *Gazette*.